THE ABSOLUTION TAP

A Unique Perspective of One Man's Battle with Depression, and the Power of Clarity, Forgiveness, and Resurrected Faith

PAUL BRISTOL

PAGE PUBLISHING, INC.
Conneaut Lake, PA

First originally published by Page Publishing 2020

ISBN 978-1-6624-0607-2 (pbk)
ISBN 978-1-6624-0608-9 (digital)

Printed in the United States of America

Absolution—Formal release from guilt, obligation, or punishment.

Tap—A device consisting of a spout and valve attached to the end of a pipe to control the flow of a fluid.

To my mother Catherine and my late father, Rock, to whom I was blessed to have been given the gift of a solid base of moral right and wrong. Despite my straying from the righteous path from time to time, to time, and many more times, their early installation of a solid road map allowed me to rediscover rather than discover my own ethical center. I was one of the lucky kids, indeed…

CONTENTS

would not have come to this decision to undertake this project without the influence of many. A major inspirational factor has been all the veterans and Gold Star family members that I have had the honor to work with via the grassroots organization I started with Scott Brown in 2011 following my father's passing. Base Camp 40—Warriors in the Wild has changed my life in ways I have yet to discover. I am in awe of the strength and fortitude exhibited by those who have been through so much but return home to turn tragedy into triumph. The example they have set has been a major inspiration in my life, for their valorous efforts continue to give back to all around them through their example of courageously overcoming so much adversity. It is a gift that has no price tag, for freedom and examples of fortitude are gifts that one can ever rightfully repay. We are a blessed nation due to those that step up to protect what we all are fortunate to have in this life. I, personally, will forever be in debt.

To my wife, Lori, my appreciation for your patience and acceptance of the time invested in my "zero-dollar contract" work with this rolling tornado known as BC40 runs deep. You have taken up the slack at home and have taken this personal devotion of mine in stride. I could not have done this without you and your love. You have been a sounding board of reason in the writing of this book, and in this life, as I always know that you will give me the straight up, not sugarcoating any feedback in order to "tell me what I want to hear." You, my dear, are a Godsend.

To Russel Redenbaugh and his book *Shift the Narrative*, I am not much of a reader of books, and I joke that before I picked up *Shift the Narrative*, the last self-help book I read was in 1991. It just so happened that it was a phone book in the Clark County, Nevada, jail where certain rut-seeking behaviors, on my behalf, produced the need for a bail bondsman. I'll admit it was helpful and a *freeing* publication nonetheless. In all seriousness, Russel's book provided clarity in the construction of the outline and map needed to complete this project. Completely different takes on this life, yet his model of what I see as changing the line of approach to landing your plane, rather than just changing your choice of runways, provided the guidance. Timing is crucial in life, so I also thank Don Lyle for introducing Russel and his book on a simple Facebook post. Right time, right place. And they say social media is full of fake news…okay, I say that, but undeniably not in this case.

To Wayne and Lana Telford, the Gold Star fathers, David Bristol, and Terry Bedford, the example you have set in your journey of living with your tragic loss is nothing short of being touched by the hand of God. Your fortitude is inspiring, and I thank you all for the example you have set for all around you.

Lastly but first, I give all glory to God and my personal savior, Jesus Christ. In all things, you will find the power of the Divine. I call it my own "beautiful, crushing, spiritual humility."

INTRODUCTION

When is the last time you met a stranger, and they asked you, "Tell me a little about yourself?" A question that is commonly answered with a name, a profession, and maybe even a hometown of origin. But how many of us really take the time to break down the process of the historic construction of our present life? For those who have lived a relatively unremarkable life, free of major loss or trauma, the need to formulate that answer beyond the level of a name and hometown probably seldom arises. But for those who find themselves struggling, at times, to get comfortable with that reflection in the mirror, it is a question that looms like the door of a principal's office before the dreaded reprimand for a third grader's misbehavior. Many, including myself, have rolled through life on the false belief that emotions are enough to explain all that needs explaining. Like the ruts in a treacherous, mountain road, we become accustomed to sliding into that low spot in the name of survival, and often subconsciously choose that route due to its predictability. If we do something long enough, we get good at it, despite its potentially destructive tendencies. It is a wicked cycle the lost and the struggling will often embrace.

In respect to that quest to honestly describe myself, I ponder another point. We all are familiar with the statement, "All men are created equal." In my opinion, this could not be further from the truth. Many individuals slide into this world with physical and mental conditions that place them on a long and tedious road, yet they accomplish the near impossible out of sheer will and fortitude. Many are also pushed out with every advantage built in, only to squander that God-given talent due to poor choices. But why the poor choices?

This pool we all swim in today is a breeding ground for opportunities to make those less-than-optimal decisions, with today's deteriorating social norms also giving individuals an endless supply of *validating crutches* on which they can prop up their bad behavior. This translates as an attempt to chalk up negative behavior as a substantiated reaction rather than a negative action that they must solely own. I have witnessed this in many adults, including the one in the mirror and the ever-growing population of entitled youth. Mental toughness is becoming a rare commodity that is being suppressed by our collective need to "feel safe and free of accountability." In many circles, personal accountability is being replaced by blame and the sterilization of our surroundings. Society has also created a model of success that places importance on financial wealth and lofty placement on the social ladder of success. These ideals are not a bad thing in themselves, but it is my opinion that true success is determined by the degree in which each individual utilizes their own personal potential, no matter how low that ceiling may be. Herein lies the contradiction. It's becoming a tougher world out there, but let's handcuff the skills of our up and coming players. Instead of building stronger players, let's just change the rules to make it easier for the weak and lazy to "have success." Destination Insanity, we have arrived. We probably need to change the phrase "when the going gets tough, the tough get going" to "when the going gets tough, the weak get more excuses, then they demand that society redefines *tough* to account for their weaknesses." In my opinion, which is what this entire book represents, we have lost our minds in the name of harmony. It's crazy, people, simply and tragically mind-boggling.

This leads to the one thing that, despite my view on our deliriously changing social expectations, I believe is the greatest potential limiting factor in our society—that being, depression. It is the opinion of this Redneck U—educated writer that depression lies at the headwaters of most destructive behaviors, such as substance abuse, eating disorders, and dysfunctional relationships (a loaded term in its own right). It's all about the escape from your present mental, emotional, and physical state, and in many cases, the baby is thrown out with the bathwater. I approach this topic from a different angle, for I minimally use the word *illness* in association with depression as it seems to stigmatize and hamstring people into limiting their own control. In my opinion, it is more so a condition, rather than an illness, that society has regarded as needing medication to be *cured*. There are different degrees and types of depression, but in the end, it is a condition that limits and hinders an individual's reach for their true potential. It is the hand that holds the key to a person's happiness in their life. Tragically, for others, it also is the hand that squeezes the trigger by which they end it.

Over the years, much light has been shed on the treatment of depression, yet we continue to have increasing rates of suicide and substance abuse in communities across the country. You see ads every day in the media that offer medical intervention, which in some cases I feel is needed, despite the side effects being almost as crippling as the condition itself. "Take this medication, and you will be able to live free, have perfect families, and get pretty chicks, despite growing a third eye on your buttocks, having to defecate twenty times a day, and have homicidal thoughts with anxiety through the roof. But you will feel better!" I have traveled that road, minus the sprints to the restroom and third eye. Wait, now that I think of it, that third eye could have been helpful in preventing my own "rectalcraniumitis." At least, maybe I would've given myself a little warning. Haha! I have gained acceptance of my own battle with what I call cyclic depression and talk about this issue, not from the perspective of my education and past work as a counselor, but as someone who lives it and has failed at dealing with it in the past. I now have "taken the reins back," so to speak, fully embracing my own neurotransmitter discombobulation that forces me to "dance with the ghost" from time to time. But I keep dancing, and that my friends, is the key to my own productive, stumbling existence.

The *Absolution Tap* is simply my journey to figuring out why I am, who I am, and who I want to be. It is not a self-help book, nor is it a guide to *get your act together*. It is just my own, at times, potentially nonsensical, collection of metaphoric models that I have found to help to break the cycle of my own rut-seeking travels. I guess I would say that this book represents my own "troubleshooting guide" in identifying why I was having bad days, bad weeks, bad months, bad years, or even bad decades. I am the sum of my parts, with each part having a role in defining my own perspective of what is good or bad. More so, it is my testament to the power/resurrection of faith in *cleaning up my own life water*. I cannot expound upon this enough, which will be detailed in the "Spiritual Tank" section of this book. Throughout, you will find that use of metaphors is one of my favorite strategies in understanding my own complex emotions and, at times, overwhelming emotional struggle. It is in the crazy power of emotions, which all originate from thoughts and cognitive sets, that we come to make or break ourselves. There is so much more to it, but we often rest on the fact that if we feel it, it must be true. In those times of emotional strife, I have found that pulling myself out of the mire to view my life "outside of my own cockpit" via an emotional metaphor construction has been invaluable and is something that I practice on a daily basis. It is not a model that just sounds good, but is a strategy that I have proven to work for me. Has it solved all my life issues? Absolutely not. It has, however, given me a chance to at least get all the lost pieces of the puzzle off the floor and onto the table. Putting it together is an ongoing and constant task.

This project is centered on the development, interaction, and impact of the "four powers within" that contribute to who we are, what we present to the world, and what we give back to ourselves. These are the Physical, Emotional, Cognitive/Intellectual, and Spiritual Tanks that we manage in every waking moment. Like the headwaters of a stream that eventually makes its way into the ocean, which through evaporation, leads to the rain that drops back on that mountain, *The Absolution Tap* takes a close look at the "water cycle of our life." Simply put, what we give to the world and to ourselves and what we allow into our tanks is the water that we all survive on. Tainted water produces tainted water, and clean water produces clean water. That statement will probably be the last clear and logical state-ment that you will read in this reflective project, so prepare for the juggling act. There will be no *eureka* moment, nor will you discover any groundbreaking conclusions. It will, however, provide a sitemap to another seat in this stadium of life to view the game that we all are witness to. As mentioned before, it is only my journey, or my seat selection, that I am sharing. I am confident that a few will find this helpful in some way, even if it delivers the reader to the conclusion that their life is not so bad compared to mine, which in the end, produces the same "I feel better about myself" outcome. Either way, mission accomplished…

Warning: They may be some colorful English utilized in this project. I believe you cannot describe a raging, charging lion in cute, playful kitten terms. Proceed at your own innocent, delicate risk!

Welcome to *the absolution tap* of my life…

The Reason for the
SELF-TREASON

A question that myself and others have asked is, What is my purpose for writing this book? I do not spend a great deal of time in figuring out why, but I would be would be remiss if I said that I didn't consider the meaning behind all this. I mean, what could possibly go wrong in opening up about all your personal struggles, leaving your past, bloodied ego bobbing in an ocean of hungry sharks? There are no critical people out there who would take great joy in taking a shot at shredding someone's attempt to help themselves and others. That's nonsense! Okay, I just climbed out from under my rock, so disregard that last Pollyannaish view. Haha! The last nine years of running a nonprofit has definitely proved that spiteful sharks in this world are far from being an endangered species. I am fully aware of the beating that this book will take, but the bottom line is that I simply don't give a rat's ass, or any other mammal's ass, in the name of being politically correct and nonbiased toward rats, about what critics will think. I am not advocating this approach for anyone, but am merely describing what works for me in keeping my own *life raft* afloat. People can dissect it all they want, but it really doesn't matter, for no one can tell me more about my journey than me, myself, and I. Too many people think they know what is best for everyone else around them, with my take being that often times the most critical are the ones who are the most out of control inside of their own war room. One of my favorite metaphors is the model of the emotional arsonist, which I will expound upon more in a later chapter. Those whose "internal houses" are ablaze will often go out and start fires in neighbor's yards just to keep the focus off their own out-of-control burn inside their own abode. I feel that is a key, subconscious coping mechanism for those who suffer from personality issues, but I will try to steer away from too much clinical jargon, as my education, training, experience, and lack of letters behind my name suggests I should not ride my horse in that arena. Sometimes thoughts and theories just find me, despite spending little time trying to figure someone out. Thoughts simply pop up for something to consider. Yes, I graduated from Cal State Northridge with a BA in psychology and worked six years in the field at a residential group home for teens and at the local hospital psychiatric ward where I did ER evaluations and facilitated group, family, and individual counseling sessions. Not all my education is from Redneck U! For the past twenty-six years, I have retained employment as a railroad engineer. Putting that education to use, by golly!

Despite myself, I have been able to lead a fairly resilient life, with many more severe *self-propelled* bullets being dodged along the way. I'm sure you have heard the saying, "A blind squirrel finds a nut every now and then." Well, my life is more like "an exposed nut that sometimes gets overlooked by that devil squirrel!" I pushed the "being a complete loser" envelope on many occasions, and by the grace of God, held it together enough to live to fight another day, time and time again. This project gave me that precious opportunity to view my fifty-six years of life from further up the mountain and embrace the perspective of viewing my journey as one of fortune, rather than one of, at times, stifling shame and disappointment. I've enjoyed each open spot on the trail to relish that view rather than be discouraged by how far I still have to travel. Simply having that opportunity to climb is a cherished gift in itself.

I supposed the most important reason for this treasonous act toward my own stumbling past is that it has been hugely beneficial to my own quest to get all those puzzle pieces off the floor. Yes, that's right. It's very self-serving and selfish. The word *selfish* in itself is deserving of some attention. Selfish. Am I really selling fish? I guess that is somewhat accurate in that I am taking what I've caught, knocked it over the head a few times and have proceeded to put it out on the market, on ice, in hopes that it doesn't spoil before someone buys it. And if it does spoil, I just hope they don't notice before I get paid! Actually, it is more like I'm providing a handbook of how one fisherman managed to get his line untangled after years of fighting the submerged, self-planted branches, and finally able to enjoy the day fishing, not necessarily catching, but just being out in it fishing. Seriously, this reflection back on how and why I struggled for so many years has been very enlightening yet trying. It is not something that I overexamine emotionally but approach it from the intellectual/ cognitive standpoint. We all have a choice in this life on how we deal with adversity, loss, and trauma. We become one of three, or even a combination of these three outcomes. We become a victim, a perpetrator/offender, or a survivor following a traumatic, life-altering experience. I have chosen to dance with all three at various times in my life. Our future is ours to define, and despite the fact that the "high road to Survivorville" is much more difficult, it still is a choice we all make. Define where you want to end up and chart your course. The road to being that survivor is paved with ownership, accountability, and a shit ton of forgiveness, courage, acceptance, and humility. The other two destinations are what many subconsciously fix their radar on, thus becoming increasingly comfortable with discomfort. More on this vicious cycle later on in this book. (You'll read, "more later in this book" quite a bit, so hang in there. I hope I remember to address it!)

Lastly, I honestly hope that this approach sheds new light for those who are struggling with finding their own pathway to that *middle lane of serenity*. When I speak with others about life struggles, particularly my own ongoing waltz with depression, I never tell anyone what to do, as I do not know their full story. When I speak with veterans, I start by telling them that I never served, therefore, I am full of it and do not know what I'm talking about. If at the end of the conversation, we are still at that juncture, then we have lost nothing, and I will support their critique. I also share that if you are depressed, it is safe to say that we both ended up in the same saloon. It's just that we rode different horses to get there, and the ride for many has been much more difficult than my own. Sharing is different from telling someone what to do. That, in my opinion, my fish-buying suckers, is the key to all lasting solutions to many of our life's quandaries.

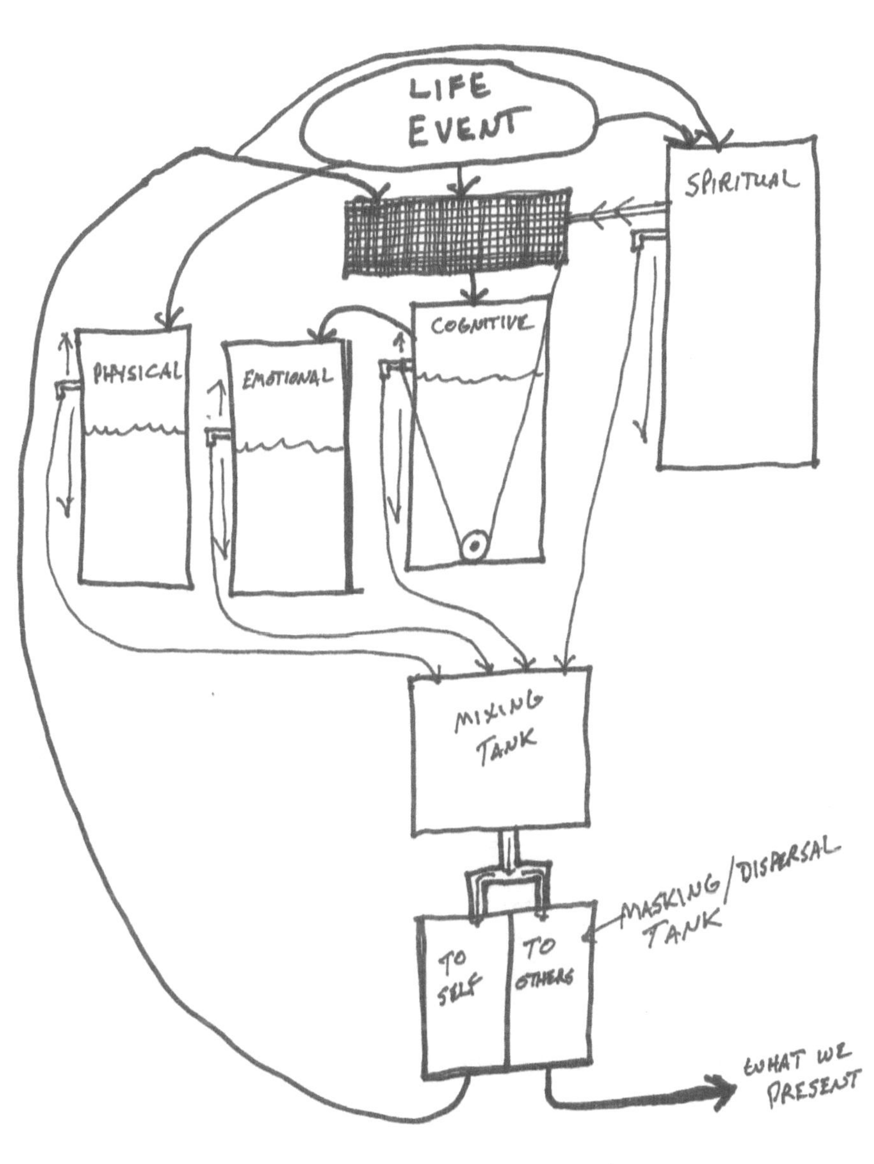
LIFE EVENT
SPIRITUAL
PHYSICAL
EMOTIONAL
COGNITIVE
MIXING TANK
MASKING/DISPERSAL TANK
TO SELF
TO OTHERS
WHAT WE PRESENT
THE TANKS!

CHAPTER 2

The Tanks of our Life

Every morning, we wake up to face another day of challenges, triumphs, failures, and other unknown obstacles that lie in wait to intervene in our lives. From our first breath, the external world begins to influence who we are and how we formulate our presentation to the world. Initially, we are totally at the mercy of our surrounding environment, with all decisions regarding our well-being residing in the hands of our parents and caregivers. This is also the beginning of the construction of the basis of this book, that being the six "tanks" that represent who we are, what we give to others, and what we recycle back to ourselves. In my own metaphoric search, I have identified these tanks to have the following labels or designations:

1. The Cognitive/Intellectual Tank
2. The Emotional Tank
3. The Physical Tank
4. The Spiritual Tank
5. The Mixing Tank
6. The Masking Phase/Final Edit

Of key importance in this model is that only one tank has the capability of having a filter installed—that being, our Cognitive/Intellectual Tank. More on this later, but if there was a *eureka* moment for me, this was it.

As we grow and mature, these *tanks* become bigger and are increasingly loaded with *environmental* water and at times, "muck," so to speak, which also leads to the increase in our ability to control what goes in each tank, the expansion of the walls, which occurs naturally with every day we live, and our choice of where we place our taps on each tank. There is much in this world that we do not have direct control over, but in the end, we all have the sole responsibility for how we react and respond to those uncontrollable floods of events, particularly those that bare the fangs of trauma and loss. The output of each tank flows to one tank where we derive our view of our own existence and what we formulate to give to the other 300-million-plus around us. Okay, maybe we are not friends of all who inhabit this country, but we all contribute to this *big river of life* via our own little tributary. We then, at times, may have the need to mask or prep the output for final dispersal. More on this later in the book.

The span of our influence through what we *put out* is as far-reaching as we choose it to be. On each end of the spectrum, our influence on the world around us increases. From extreme evil and destructive acts to extreme compassion and the divine drive to give back to others, all of us are found somewhere on that impact scale. I would venture to guess that most find themselves somewhere in the middle. Where we land on that grid is our choosing, end of story. If you would *test your own water*, where would it fall on this life-impact scale? A question not asked enough of ourselves, with my own revelation of the answer to this question providing the motivation to take my baby steps toward making positive changes in my own life.

Social media in this country has become a breeding ground for the destructive, negativity-laced force that has everyone passing judgment, like it's gas that is passed after a bean burrito eating contest. Since the Big River is dirty, what will it hurt to add a little more to it? Hypocrisy has found a new gear, for sure, as this country continues to divide itself over issues that we think we know but really know very little about. That's why I have chosen, quite some time ago, to bow out of this negativity campaign. So much more positive things that exist in this life that I choose to dedicate my time and effort to. Here is my recent social media post on this topic:

As a human being, what makes up the definition of self? It is my opinion that we have lost our compass in the fog of drama, mistaking characteristics and interests with what should be of most importance—that being, what lies at our moral center. The following is what I think we are not:

We are not gay or straight, black or white, or skinny or fat. We are not liberal or conservative, American or Russian, or a fighter or a pacifist. We are not Christian or atheist, Muslim or Jew, or hunter or vegan. Many have lost their way, clinging to the characteristic that best allows for the victim persona, thus giving a crutch to self-righteous anger and hate in the name of *defending the cause*. Technology has allowed for this easy expression of the indecent in the new "not okay corral of the new Wild, Wild Web," replacing pistols with PCs, swords with smart phones, and bullets with brash tweets. It's a coward's carnival at our fingertips. What we have lost is the real definition of what matters—that is, full ownership of what lies in our soul and what good we cast into the societal mix. We have cherry-picked what characteristic serves our reeling desires best in that hedonistic moment, pushing kindness and humility, not only to the back burner but off the stove altogether. We must lose the masks and return to those things that don't get votes or summon mob mentality. It is the part of our reflection in our mirrors that we shy away from because that image demands accountability and change. We are all human, and we are all sinners. We must begin the process of acknowledging such before those mirrors are banned altogether, thus giving free rein to forces beyond our control.

It is truly a fight for individual civility, thus leading to the salvation of a civil population. Heed the warning signs, we must...

Now that the squirrel has disappeared back into the treetop, back to the tanks...

My sister Jeanne and I

The Early Construction

I had initially written a well-thought-out recollection of my past, providing much detail about how my own tanks were constructed and influenced by both external and internal forces. After reading over it many times, I came to the realization that this book is not so much about me, but more about the process and the golden lessons learned. I will keep this section simple and to the point.

I was blessed to be raised by two imperfect perfect parents who did their very best to ensure success for my sister and I (five years older). It is in reflection where it became clear my father battled depression the old-school way, which was a pattern that I subconsciously replicated in my own adulthood, in detail. But through it all, we knew we were loved and supported, and we were raised in a rural farm setting that taught us the importance of hard work and appreciation for life. Surrounded by animals, the fortitude to survive losing something you love was religiously instilled on that farm, and the respect for those creatures that we share this earth with was deeply embedded. I was a fortunate kid in many ways, with this respect and compassion for life only increasing over the years. Yes, I am a hunter, but do so with an ever-present respect and humility for that gift of the harvest.

I will admit that in my early years, I was extremely shy and withdrawn, which led to the development of a very vivid imagination in my attempts to entertain myself. In regards to that tank building, we were instilled with clear boundaries and discipline, which in retrospect, probably was my saving grace as I ventured into the land of needing to escape my own skin via my own self-destructive behavior. My parents did their job, so no crutch to carry forward. The importance of education, the exposure to Christianity, and their encouragement and steadfast support in pursuing our passions in sports and equine competition made for an early tank construction that we were fortunate to be given. I often use the phrase "the hardest beds I've lain in are the ones I've made myself." So true is this for me.

It is in this early construction that we are the most vulnerable and without adequate defense mechanisms to properly deal with the influence of our outer world. It can set the stage for later life struggles, but only if it is allowed to rule without correction. Just because it happened, it doesn't mean that it still has to happen. Many forfeit their present-day control to their past, but our past is only relevant when we choose to give it defining authority. We tend to empower our past due to the lack of tools, tools that we often choose not to search for. This is also one of the main reasons that I am sharing my experiences. Hopefully, it will serve as example that change is possible, no matter how long one has driven in those deep ruts of brutal predictability. If you want something better, you will find it. If you are comfortable in the struggle, then that is probably where you will stay, for no one can do it for you. There is always hope and a better way out there for the willing to discover.

CHAPTER 4

The Meaning Behind the Metaphors

Despite my fortunate upbringing, for years I wandered through this existence searching for that elusive, lasting inner peace. Having the realization at around age twenty-four that I was indeed depressed (my former self-appointed, ignorant title of a semi-educated analyst told me this), I began the subconscious search of finding a way out of this dark, periodic well. My depression is cyclic, so I was provided the needed breaks that pulled me out of *the mire* to once again breathe a little easier, despite my own self-medicating efforts that only exacerbated the issue. When my taps would plummet, and the lines would become clogged, why not mix in a little alcohol and stir it up, just in the name of getting *something* to come out? This became an ever-repeating cycle as I would come out of what I call the Well Bottom just long enough to see the carnage of what I had accomplished while in that deceptive swamp. That would then provide the subconscious motivation to go right back in, for in the Well Bottom, life is really pretty easy. It was emotionally destructive but a low, easy road all the same. Throughout this book, I will give reference to my own depression and it's, at times, smothering influence on my life, but allow me to make one thing crystal clear. None of this is a crutch to validate *any* innocence for *any* of *my* bad decisions. I am totally responsible for my own failures. There's no one to blame, and nothing else to hold accountable; no matter what has happened along the way, I *always* had a choice, and I *always* knew the right thing to do. Once I truly embraced this shitty and, at times, tough-to-digest accountability role, my life began to change. About nine years ago, this process definitely caught another gear. I gathered all the "ugliness of my past into one room" and owned it all. My favorite metaphor for this process is that I gathered up all my players onto the team bus, only to revisit some pretty shady teammates. But what is of most importance in this crowded bus is who I allow behind the wheel to chart my course in this life. It doesn't matter who my eternal riders are, but it is who I choose to drive my bus that matters most, and I make that decision every morning when I start my day. That process of choosing the driver, in my opinion, is determined by two things. One is the spiritually appraised value that I have on the contents of my bus. And two, the predictability and familiarity of who I have in my *pool of drivers*. More on this in a later chapter as well. All of this accountability provided a solid start to getting my thoughts, emotions, and spiritual beliefs into their proper perspective. It now occurs without much second thought, but not without occasional, brief slides back into the old perspective, which demands several passes through that newly reformed cognitive/intellectual filter. You could say that I redefined, reconstructed, and rediscovered what was, and is, rote for me. Yes, I still wrestle with being affected at times by others and my own negative inclinations, but I have found the awareness to reel it back into that middle lane in which clarity of thought resides. I have to admit, change that is lasting is incredibly difficult. I compare it to my own past experience in working with teens who sabotage their own progress after a weekend home visit with their family. They tiptoe out on that ledge of recovery, only to slide back into their old destructive mindsets in the name of belonging. Even though they made strides in their own personal journey, their family's position did not move therefore creating a sense of alienation. I can't even imagine the sense of abandonment that unfortunately comes with a fragile teens' emotional struggle. I find it somewhat similar in making changes within in my own *internal family*. It has to be a systems approach, for if I simply address the deficiencies of one area, it is easy to slide back into that old, destructive rut. I had to address every member or tank and make it a holistic effort. This was key to at least turning the corner to permanently changing my life perspective, or as Russel Redenbaugh states, "Changing my narrative." I had to revive and embed my spiritual conviction, renew my drive to being healthier physically (an ongoing process), and discover the differentiation between past and present emotional and intellectual issues. It is like the foggy window to that healthier perspective has been wiped clean, and now I am cranking that window open to start to breathe that new air. The abandonment of old ways can be trying, and at times, alienating, but once, I merely brushed against that inner, emotional, spiritual calm, that's all it took. I now know it exists and find myself cranking that window open a little more each day. Therein lies the weight of accountability and discovery. Hope and faith quells that sense of abandonment that comes with changing your old cognitive and emotional launch pads. To describe it as powerful and liberating is an understatement, but man, it is hard, persistent work. With it comes awareness, which demands action. No more claiming ignorance. It is a positive challenge that I am thankful to be presented with. Here is my recent social media post on this topic:

> They say old habits die hard, but old beliefs and past negative mindsets, well, they never die. You just have to constantly adjust and tighten the gag in order to keep them out of your present-day conversation! For me, negative thoughts/mindsets are like that bolt of lightning where emotions represent the ensuing roll and boom of thunder. Just take the time to make sure your initial interpretation or *strike* is accurate and true in its aim. It is in that misinterpretation that I, at times, had a tendency to turn that raindrop into a raging storm.

Years ago, even after finding that balance does exist, I still wanted more for my own happiness. I have gone the medication route (fifteen years ago), and that didn't work out too well. Depression alleviated, but the anxiety went through the roof. At that time, I already had that predisposition to want to punch every "thinking about being a smartass" man in the mouth, and the medication route only made that a more easily reached conclusion. It was like giving a shark a shot of blood to help calm them down. Not for me, so it was back to alcohol and skirt chasing/catching. That old rut was once again occupied. Cost versus return. It was a crazy cycle that I repeated over and over again, for many years. All through this, I maintained a semiresponsible life. Looking back, I had, at times, a tendency to sabotage the right decisions simply because they were not sexy enough and lacked the adrenaline pump that came from bar fighting and schmoozing with one of God's most amazing creations—that being, women. During this time of pseudo, convenient answer-seeking behavior, I made four trips to the various law enforcement drop-off facilities in various and not-to-be-named parts of the country. But in every confrontation with Mr. Lawman, which preceded the free ride to the common senseless shelter, I always shut 'er down, no matter how rageful or *alcoholically overmedicated* I found myself to be. That was for sure my early-in-life, instilled respect for authority hunkering down through the twister. My "never cross" zone also included physically striking any woman, no matter what had emitted out of their—at times, proficient and vengeful communication portal. Once again, thank you, Jesus and my parents, for that upbringing.

Regarding this tank model, you could say that it found me for the most part. God has blessed me with the gift of creativity, which at times can be distracting because I see life as one giant, constantly running, play on words. I'm sure there may be a professional or two out there that reads this and draws the conclusion that I am bipolar, but that's an explanation that I have considered and dismissed. No episodes of mania where I can go without sleep and get lots done in the process. Sorting out what is my baseline has been somewhat troubling over the years, as I'll admit my swings presented questions about this possibility. I am pretty confident that my ups are simply when I've been pulled out of the well. When you spend as much time in that well as I have, the time above ground can really take on a greater significance. Over elation, at times, to be above ground, but not to the extent of being manic.

As I mentioned before, metaphors serve as a go-to tool to make sense of the twisted. Getting above the fray to change my perspective is something that I have proven to myself that I am never stuck. There will always be options, even though it may only be an option to change the perspective and not the scene. Sometimes that is all I need to get through to the next day where I will eventually find my way. I am never stuck, just temporarily assigned to the mud pit. This tank view has been a product of that constant perspective search, and for me, it has proven to be a very practical approach. I initially had plans to write a book called *The Well Bottom Bar and Grill*, which also addressed the topics of the four tanks, but the tank model emerged as the most easily followed (I know, this will be hard to follow, so imagine what that storyline would have been!) I will be using some of that content because it also accurately describes what goes on in my head during those "visits to well." I believe that the key in this happiness-seeking quest is to answer the question of why I am feeling a certain way and educating myself on how I arrived at the station of emotional discomfort. I equate this to learning about how my vehicle works and mastering the task of troubleshooting when it breaks down on the side of the road. I see many settling for the "feeling of being stranded," with no clear plan to get their ride back up and rolling, which leads to them blaming their mechanic (whom they themselves chose), other drivers for not stopping to help, and the condition of this highway of life itself. For years, I failed to even acknowledge that my truck was not hitting on all cylinders, let alone opening the hood to answer the question of why it wasn't running correctly. Educating myself on *the why* didn't rid me of all my issues, but it was incredibly empowering when I sorted out how I ended up tapped at the bottom of my tank, thus giving way to a clearer plan on how to move it back above the muck line. I then travel on until the next temporary challenge, or depressive swing, that arises. Really comforting in those low times, this awareness has provided.

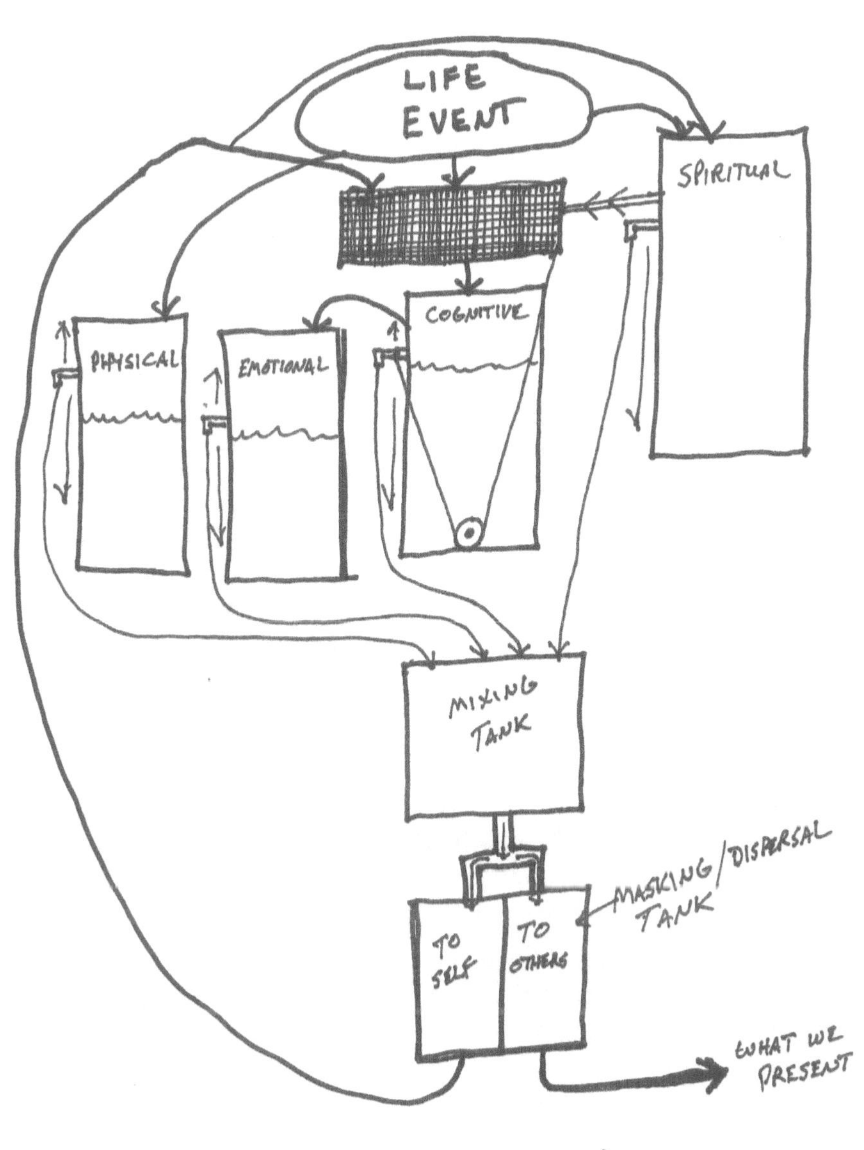

LIFE EVENT
SPIRITUAL
PHYSICAL
EMOTIONAL
COGNITIVE
MIXING TANK
MASKING/DISPERSAL TANK
TO SELF
TO OTHERS
WHAT WE PRESENT
THE TANKS!

CHAPTER 5

The Plumbers' Nightmare

The following model is simply my own view of what goes into the production of what I put out to those around me and recycle back to myself. I will attempt to describe this process via diagrams and the following *one-way* written dialogue. Along the way, I will describe what happens when I have erred in the proper tank management, which I think is the crux of this entire metaphoric model. If you find yourself lost in this presentation, just think, you could be me! Haha! Walk a mile in my shoes, and you may just end up on the side of a milk carton. I will leave as many markers as possible for you, the reader, to follow. Just don't take your eyes off the road or operate heavy machinery after reading these segments. Lets' get going…

As I mentioned before, I have concluded that I control what I put into my tanks, where I choose to place my taps and, through life events, the size of my tanks. What is processed out of the cognitive/ intellectual filter into that Intellectual/Cognitive Tank directly determines what is passed into that Emotional Tank. All then flows to the final *mixing phase*, then onto the *masking tank* for prep to be presented to others. Major trauma and loss results in that uncontrollable, vat-filling dump, and that line-clogging *muck* is there forever. I then have a choice. I can, over time, learn to live with that muck at the bottom, thus letting it settle to where I can discover the clarity of the separation, or I can continue to keep it mixed-up via self-destructive behavior. That continual mixing of the sludge produced an ongoing flow of tainted water that then lead to my inability to even recognize the clean water that would normally rise to the top. That's where in the past I got into trouble and found my life unrecognizable. Substance abuse is a key player in this *power-mixing* process but is not the only "spoon in the tank." Isolation, narcissism, passive-aggressive behavior, and aggression toward self and others support that avoidance of identifying exactly what my tanks have been tainted with, and it is here where the race between denial and honest introspection hits the track.

In regards to where we place our taps, that is a choice we all make. Although depression attempts to force our taps to the bottom below the clean-water level, we still can battle our way up to move that connection. It is through the strength of my Spiritual Tank that I now move those taps back just above the sludge line, which, in my opinion, is where a majority of people find their taps. When all taps are perceived to have bottomed out and nothing comes out due to the line being blocked from within, that is when one finds themselves at the end of the line, and taking one's own life becomes the perceived only way out. The low point of my life came seventeen years ago when I threatened to do just that during a drunken rage. That was my rock-bottom moment. That was when I came face to face with all that I had haunted myself with and all that I had chosen to hang on to. Completely submerged in that victim's pool, consequently finding myself drowning in my own self-pity. This is the first time I have "been out" with this incident and shared this episode with my present wife soon after writing it down. At that time, all my self-induced shame was on the table, and a decision had to be made. I now thank the Lord for giving me the resolve to make the right turn. As mentioned before, I have always stood by the saying that "the hardest beds I've lain in are the ones I made myself." I guess I always thought that, but for the longest time, I mistakenly interpreted that as a slogan for my own campaign for self-pity, at least up until that moment of contemplating and verbalizing this *ticket to permanent purgatory*. The seed to recovery was planted in the middle of the night in the midst of that devastating deluge of out-of-control thoughts and emotion. It took another seven years for the plant to show signs of growth, but I am certain that is when real change was given its roots, as well as when I was blessed with my undeniable divine intervention on a Utah highway in 1987. More on this personal, spiritual pillar-producing experience in the "Spiritual Tank" chapter.

I often hear people state this when referencing their past: "I am a different person now." I could not disagree more with this line of thinking. Our mindsets and image of ourselves may drastically improve, but every negatively impactful decision we make stays with us, residing at the bottom of our tanks. A wounded, destructive, and repressed lion leads to a vicious lion given potential to come back to haunt. I know that I am the same person, it's just that I have permanently armed myself with the hope, faith, accountability, and the forgiveness to keep these man stalkers at a distance and out of the cognitive narrative of my present life. I am who I am and who I used to be. I believe that embracing, accepting, and forgiving *all* the roles I played all throughout my past has proven to be the surest way to come to grips with all that contributed to "mucking up" my tanks. This resolution has entrenched my "lion securement check," thus keeping all in a proper, awareness-driven perspective.

In the following sections, I will introduce a brief history of the contents of *my tanks*. And yes, I will be repetitive throughout this book, so consider it a means to helping you stay on track. It appears quite complex, but it really became pretty simple once I cut through all the excuses that I've used to subconsciously rationalize my own, at times, less-than-admirable behavior. Let me start with the easiest to understand, the Physical Tank.

THE PHYSICAL TANK!

The Physical Tank

Perhaps the most straightforward tank of the four—the Physical—represents just that. It is the natural development, maintenance, and eventual breakdown of our physical selves. There is no filtering inside this tank, but we do have a great deal of control in what we load it with. Most of my life I have been pretty athletic, with most of my success in sports being due to drive and work ethic, not natural, freakish physical tools and ability.

Baseball was my sanctuary for many years, as all was quiet within during the time on the mound/ diamond. All-State Honorable Mention as a senior in high school, State and Regional American Legion Tournament MVP in 1982, and more importantly, as a team, Regional Champions and a third place finish in the American Legion World Series that summer with a team ran and funded by Gene Taylor. Geno had a profound impact on my confidence, as well as being an influence in my present-day drive to give back to others. Another father figure that I know will never be forgotten by many in this community. I was fortunate to have the sport pay for two years of my college, so it was a plus for my parents. My parents were steadfast in their support, never missing a game through my high school years. At home, they helped me develop those skills, as both caught for me during my backyard bullpen sessions between ages eight to twelve. My mother, who used to be a fast pitch softball catcher, retired her role when I was twelve, when I snapped off a wicked twelve-to-six curve ball," which broke her big toe. I remember hours of playing "flip" and "21" with my dad in the evenings after he completed his work on the farm, as he always made time for that. I have really great memories of that time.

Genetics play a major role, as well, in determining what makes it out to the final, end tap of that Physical Tank. We are all born with a physical skill/characteristic set, and our bar setting should be constructed around what we have and not what others possess. As mentioned before, much of my life I have been pretty active, even in times of being a bit okay, at times, extremely overweight. Yes, I have dumped some pretty tainted water into this vat, water that contained lots and lots of alcohol. Almost two years ago, I quit drinking altogether, just simply quit. One of my former tank-polluting cohorts/ room renters asked me a few months ago if I was still on the wagon. I told her, "No, I'm on a totally different road, and I'm walking it, so no need for a wagon." We dump these mind-altering substances into multiple tanks, for one reason and one reason only. It's because it feels better than the sober alternative and, in some cases, helps us avoid facing the uncomfortable image in the mirror. Cost versus return once again raises its ugly presence. The more we do it, the easier it gets to overindulge in the spirits because we subconsciously chip away at our value of self. Maybe that is why I do not believe in antidepressant drugs for myself, as well. Not saying that others may benefit, but I'm not convinced that it is the best answer for myself to feel better. I'm sure the multibillion-dollar pharmaceutical industry differs with me, but man, once again, what about those ads? You may feel less depressed, but you may experience increased feelings of wanting to harm yourself, increased feelings of wanting to kill someone else, and maybe even grow an eyeball out of your posterior. I guess that would be the true definition of hindsight! No, thank you, I will take my depression in a straight, predictable shot. Plus, I need no rear view eye in that location as I've had my head in that area for much of my life. Don't need another reminder.

Three years ago, I was diagnosed with AFib, a heart condition that both my parents were diagnosed with. My sister recently recalled those moments during our hunting trips with our father, moments where he would just sit down under a tree to rest, for no apparent reason. My own journey has led me to being medication free, despite still having occasional episodes that I just ride out. I remember being placed on a certain medication a few years ago, a medication that I proceeded to do some research on soon after I started taking it. (This was kinda like picking up a flight manual to fly a plane for the first time and reading it after I've already taken off! Haha!) Every medical article I read stated, "Do not prescribe for AFib." After speaking with the cardiologists' nurse about this revelation, her response was that many doctors are prescribing it, so it is okay to ignore the manufacturer's warning? Once again, I will take it straight up, for I feel in my case, the medication was doing more harm than good. Battle forward, on my own terms…

Throughout my life, I placed a high priority on being able to physically complete the task, even in times when I shouldn't have even tried something. As a pitcher that always had to run, I ran a 5:04/ mile, and even completed a mini triathlon at age forty-three. The Physical Tank tap was wide open, until one day 4 years ago when it all changed. I've had several broken bones, but the day I ruptured my left quad tendon while hiking on the mountain, this became a life-altering event that changed my life…for the better. This was followed by a mandatory right hip replacement three months after the quad repair. I've battled with that hip issue since I was a pitcher in high school and gutted it out until it was a necessity, and a mandate from my quad surgeon to fix it. Many have stated that the location on the mountain where it happened must now hold a bad memory. Probably the greatest pain I have ever experienced, tumbling through the rocks after blacking out, ending up with a dislocated patella and an obvious gap where my inner quad tendon should have been. From my perspective, that place gives me a sense of comfort, as I would have been above ten thousand feet on a veterans' wilderness elk hunt two weeks later if it hadn't ruptured when and where it occurred. A huge opening in that life-altering storm cloud, for sure. I rest easy with this position on that incident.

I couldn't have turned this into a positive without my having met thirty-year-old retired army captain Jeremy Linn in 2013 on a BC40 cow elk hunt here in Colorado. I was blessed to be witness to his four-day lesson on human perseverance as Jeremy was in full battle with liver and esophageal cancer. His outlook was "I don't have cancer. Cancer has me. I'm going to live my life on my own terms." He passed away, on his own terms, four and half months after his successful cow elk hunt. A deep, soul-impacting impression this man made on my life. A similar impact was made three years ago by USMC veteran Eric Hughes. At age thirty, he was given six weeks to six months to live after extensive treatment for an aggressive form of brain cancer. He planned his funeral with his father but vowed to stay alive to see the birth of his daughter. Well, he made that goal and raised the bet with cancer 4 years, and today, continues to battle forward. There's another soul-shifter that I have been blessed to have met. His example of hitching his wagon to only what's positive has been a testament to his faith and inner fortitude, thus raising the importance of that Spiritual Tank influence. The status of the tumors is now going on five years of no growth/no movement. A miracle is what this guy represents, and yes, there is his beard. Yeah, it's gotta have something to do with the mojo in that beard…

After my fortunate incident, I found myself unable to ever run or jog again, and my high-country elk hunting would have to be put on hold. Because of Jeremy's gift, I never once got down about it. I simply adjusted my perspective, despite this potentially overwhelming sludge dump into my Physical Tank. I moved my tap up the ladder to keep it out of the mire, thus focusing on the things I could do and the new challenges presented. I filtered it out of the Intellectual/Emotional Tanks, for no solution could be derived from running that incident through those routes. Not as much pressure in that line as before, but small gains have huge impacts if you stay focused on what lies ahead, and not on what could have been. We all will start that slowdown/breakdown process of physical aging, but we still can choose where we tap into that tank. I have focused on what is working and left what I used to do out of the mix. Deal with what you have, gear down, and crawl your way up the mountain. It does no good whatsoever to fret over the "cant's in life." When faced with life-altering conditions, it is easy to allow our perspective to sink below the surface. Just stay above the sludge, adjust your expectations, and climb on.

I have to admit that depression has a major impact on that Physical Tank as well. It is a neurotransmitter issue and can have other physical effects because of that neurotransmitter imbalance. Keeping that in mind during those times is key for me in my awareness and self-education of this outlook-altering process. Awareness and clarity once again play a major role in the process of damage control when depression drops like a heavy blanket spun out of the wool of the "I don't give a damn" sheep. I have found that diet has had a noticeable impact during these trips to "the well," for cutting out what depression orders up is like physically starving it out from all the feel-good foods that support its presence in the room. At the time, I started this literary project, I had dropped fifty pounds through diet alone but seemed to have found all that I had lost over two years' time. I have found that it has to be a holistic weight-loss plan, with the discipline coming in the form of eating all-natural foods (what I can kill or pick with a stick), eliminating alcohol altogether (that was an easy one since I rarely drank at the time I quit), and just having a better overall outlook on the clarity of my life in general. The Physical Tank has taken a beating over the years, but it still is holding strong despite the barrage of garbage that I have loaded it with throughout my life. I never know when it will take a dive into the ditch, but I choose to take it as it comes, and be thankful every day for what is still keeping me upright. Tap above the muck, and battle forward, people, battle forward…

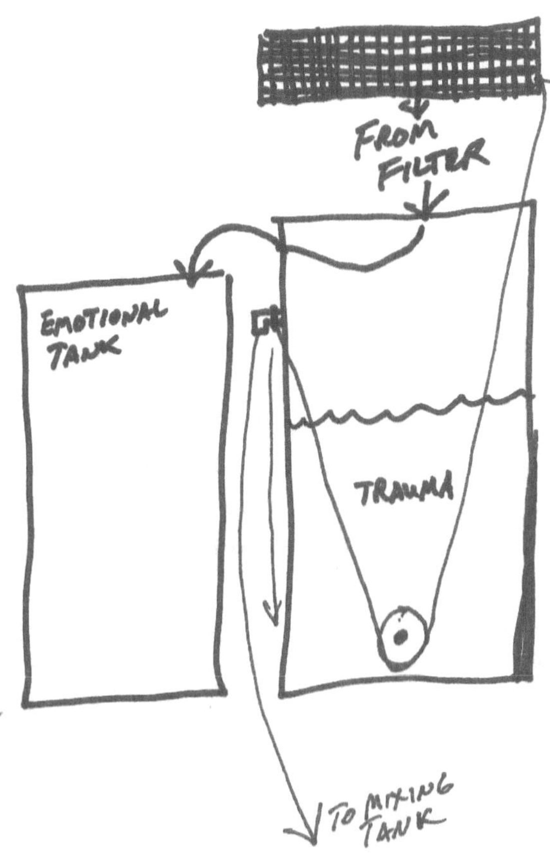

THE COGNITIVE / INTELLECTUAL TANK!

The Cognitive/Intellectual Tank

How many times have you heard from others or said to yourself, "What were you thinking?" For me, that question was presented far too many times, by both myself and others. And the answer to this question, well, I wasn't so much thinking as I was feeling. Simple as that, giving free reign to emotions, without proper filtering. The tainted intellectual filter had already sent the negative self-image memo, then proceeded to take a seat in the shadows to watch the ensuing emotional quagmire take shape. It's shit-slinging at its finest, with the end product reassuring the intellectual filter rep that he was right all along. Self-fulfilling prophecies I certainly and religiously adopted. With every self-imploding thought, I chopped away at that self-esteem, as I had gone all in amid this game of "looking to lose at poker." Hedonism became the fallback reward regardless of the cost. Here in this tank lies a great deal of control, folks. It is the "second in command" in my life, for when I completely bought in, intellectually/cognitively, the result transpired, good or bad, depending on the theme of my show at the time. In the revelation of that cognitive filter is where I have found that pot of gold in this search. Let's say you have a rope attached to your intellectual tank tap, with that rope running to a pulley at the bottom of your tank, then back up to the filter. That filter is like the strings of a tennis racket. When the tap is high above the *muck line* on the Cognitive Tank, those strings on the filter are tight, thus allowing a more effective filtering of daily experiences that you can prevent from *dropping* into your tank, unedited. It is straight, tight, and right that we seek. Once that tap is lowered by depression, the filter is loosened, thus allowing more negative events to slip through without proper review. Herein lies that double-edged sword that depression wields. I've been pushed down into the garbage of my past, and now have to deal with my semidefenseless coping of everyday life events. Getting that tap back above the mire to access that cleaner water is vital to limiting the compounding power of depression. I am still working on securing the tightness of those strings in that filter, tying them off, so to speak. Swinging that pulley connection from the Cognitive/Intellectual Tank to the Spiritual

Tank provides for that string tightness in the low times, resulting in the ability to maintain that, at times dim, positive perspective. I believe that this is the battleground where those who take their own life find their endgame. Once I can remove that rope and pulley from the mix, I will have hit a major milestone in this ongoing education about this crazy process. Simply put, this Intellectual Tank is what I think, the Emotional Tank is how I feel about what I think, and the intellectual filter determines why I think it. See, that's not so hard to follow…if you stop right here.

This tank has the most responsibility of all the tanks in regards to accountability, for my thoughts and mindsets have determined the trajectory of my life and the emotions that ensue. I've heard people say, "I was feeling really angry so that's why I lashed out." But the million-dollar question is, What was the precipitating, deeply entrenched mindset/narrative that opened the door for that knee-jerk, negative emotion? If anyone takes anything out of this book, I hope it's this. My mindset or cognitive narrative of my life (thank you, Russel!) set the stage for the birth, rise, and/or suppression of my negative and positive emotions. That, perhaps, paired with my spiritual reconnection is the Holy Grail that I have discovered in getting my life back on track. Negative mindsets and the fixture onto others negativity create more volatile and more easily reachable, destructive emotions. I know this is not a new theory, but I cannot stress this enough. These mindsets got their start early in life (no fault of my parents, I would add), and without any path correction, lead on into adulthood. It is in adulthood where I solidified and deepened those rut tracks, and the more I traveled in that low spot, the more it became second nature. Diminished value results in decreased investment to improve one's position. Now those that have known me may be saying, "I don't remember him being very negative," but what you see is not always what lies in the altered tank water of what you get. Once again, enter the masking phase, which I was really good at. I lost that sense of needing to reevaluate "upstream" as the deeper I got, the better I became at altering the output, rationalizing the irrational. The dirty water cycle just kept on rolling. This desperation to dodge the responsibility ball lasted for many years, until, as I mentioned before, I needed better answers for myself. I often surrounded myself with like individuals, for as author John Bradshaw puts it, "Chess players don't hang out with hockey players because they don't know the rules." This made it easier to choose not to look for better answers, as belonging truly loves familiar company. Those around me were not to blame, but it did simplify the choice of diving deeper into the mire. I love those friends from childhood like brothers, for they helped me through some pretty rough times. A few had a front-row seat to my *chaotic show* but never gave up their spot during the melee. They are examples that further support my view that in my life I have been extremely fortunate and blessed. In regards to my own dysfunctional mindset, my desire to change led to my conviction to empty out that leftover, waterproof gunpowder and TNT that I held onto for emergencies in times of subconsciously needing to feel sorry for myself. Absolutely nuts, if you ask me…

Injection of self into less-than-optimistic/doomed-to-fail relationships is a horse that I seemed to eagerly throw my saddle onto in order to desperately improve that cognitive image of self. Subconsciously, I entered up into these boat races like a "knight in tinfoil armor with a canoe…with gaping holes in it…with no oars… and no life jackets," and I was crushed when I found my vessel at the bottom of the lake halfway through the trip. I will touch on these relationship dynamics later on, but now looking back, man, what a strong indicator of just how ignorantly and arrogantly I approached relationships. Cost versus return and the filling of a gaping void that no external factor could ever fill. Many times, the return was the entrenchment of the "narrative of the victim" launching point in my own life. I was quite the rescuer (a setup), for I embraced the thought that I could "make someone's life better," thus the multiple relationships I had with single mothers. On the face of it, it appeared rather gallant and genuinely caring. In hindsight, however, it was an unrealistic and subconsciously pompous view in thinking I could load up a woman and her child onto my flailing canoe, and all would be okay. As long as I dove headfirst into this "knight in tinfoil armor" role (hey, it was still shiny!), maybe then I could find value in myself. That was the reality that I was unable to see and detect through the layer of denial of my own issues. Some may not believe this, for why would someone do that to themselves and others? Depression attacks full force on this battleground and easily can turn a perceived gallant effort into a struggle for survival in the "deep part of the lake" as it is also the master at creating internal deception. This also touches on the internal versus external locus of control that I found myself engaged with, one side or the other. Did I just say engaged with? I was obviously a Master Jedi in that "starship premarriage battle-group" (yes, I'm on my fourth marriage)…just wasn't very good at saving those particular galaxies after the ceremony. Yes, I know some of my smartass friends will say something like, "No it was the size of your lightsaber that caused your defeat!" Just thought I'd better beat them to the punch! More on this dynamic in a different chapter.

Where I decide to tap into this tank is also affected by what is predictable. A great challenge indeed, even when I internalized the positive progress made. I know I am repeating this thought, but it is worth repeating. Sliding back into those old ruts is so easy to do and carries heavier weight once you have attained that clarity of what needs to be done. Clarity and accountability force the issue of better decisions but is still subject to the slide into the "comfortable discomfort." The effort in recovering from those times of self-doubt has definitely gained a weapon via the act of forgiving myself for the temporary regression, as well as seeking divine forgiveness for the return to the mire. In the power of forgiveness is where I discovered that this tank model really does make sense and is more than just a good idea. Being able to maintain that rational perch during the storm is liberating to say the least.

It is through the influence of this Intellectual Tank where recovery is more about educating myself and addressing thoughts rather than controlling emotions. You take away the destructive narrative, then lo and behold, the negative emotional output decreases. I found that I am my own worst enemy, not those who commit less-than-admirable acts directed my way. In humbling and educating myself of my own destructive narrative production, the entire battlefield became much clearer. The battle continues every day, but when I gained control of my own troops and clearly identified what I will not accept from others (once again, thank you, Mr. Redenbaugh), the plan of attack became much more rational in thought rather than the knee-jerk, improperly filtered emotional response that resulted in my voluntarily relinquishment of ground to those attempting to take it. But those deep, inviting ruts will always be there. Knowing where they are and how to get out of them is more than half the battle.

In brief summation of this Intellectual Tank description, it all is set by that filter at the top, where all life events get sorted and labeled. In this breeding ground for all emotions, it is here where we create our long-term vision of our lives. This is what we see when we are alone and determine if our life is worth saving via, at times, unpopular, unfamiliar, and steep choices. Out of the Emotional Tank comes the loudest voice in the room, but it is in the Intellectual Tank where that script is written, influenced by the narrative-defining cognitive filter. Do we blame the dramatic actor or the undermining script-writer when our life scenes go awry? Something for myself to ponder every waking moment, for sure…

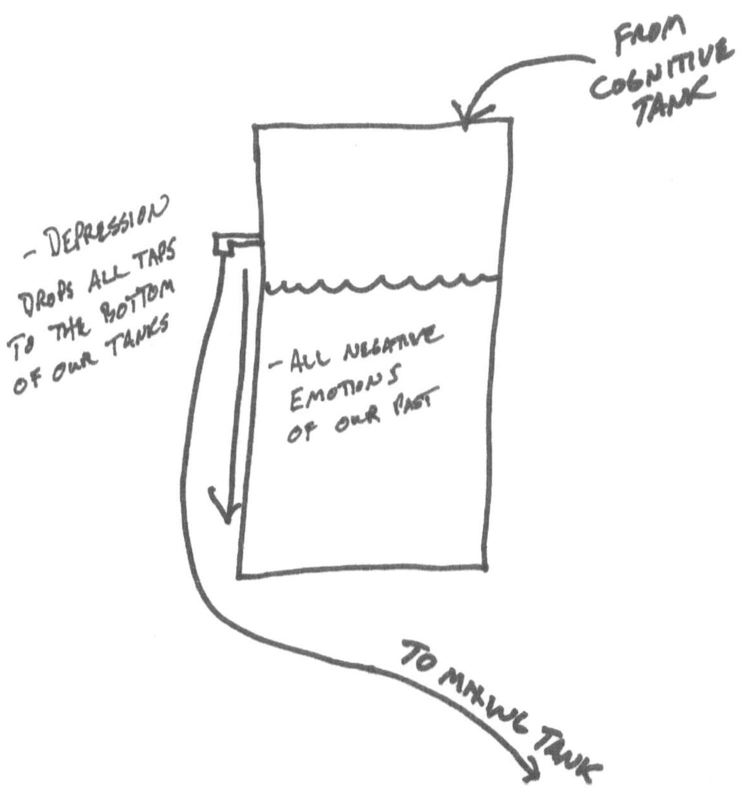

THE EMOTIONAL TANK!

The Wildcat in the Water—a.k.a. the Emotional Tank

Here in this section lies the source of my most destructive nemesis of my past—that being, the activity in the Emotional Tank. Generally speaking, emotions have so much power on this rock of humanity. They can be the most beautiful force that moves mountains in the form of love; compassion; and true, heartfelt sympathy and can deeply change the lives of all who engage. It creates indescribable joy and puts beautiful value on why we do kind things for others during our time above ground. Unfortunately, it also can tear apart lives from the inside out and keep one segregated from the aforementioned bliss that we all seek. It is a creator and a destructor, a mover and a paralyzer, and be a source of both powerful inspiration and of utter and complete destruction of one's soul, when left unchecked. For much of my adult life, unchecked was my emotional interpretation of my life events. It was the boat afloat with no anchor in this rolling sea, which resulted in the development and progression of a defense mechanism that many choose to build their "life crutch" out of—that being, the rise of the victim. At times, so subtle in its growth while at other times, being the monster coming out of the ocean to wreak havoc on all on the surrounding beach. I go back to the metaphor of the "my team that's on the bus" as it just simply makes sense. When I internalized that it doesn't matter who I've been emotionally in the past but who is now driving the bus, that is when the course correction occurred. All those past players are still aboard in their respective seats, which includes those wearing the jerseys of rage, jealousy, spite, and insecurity, just to name a few. When I finally planted the spiritual player behind the wheel, despite the others begging to drive at times, that was surely a moment of defining clarity. And who assigns the drivers? The Intellectual Tank, of course, determined by the makeup of that Intellectual Tank filter.

For many years, I adopted the common course of action of letting those emotions ride and let the chips fall where they may, regardless of the destruction it created. Without that positive filter in place over the Intellectual Tank, negativity-laced narratives were free to flow directly into my Emotional Tank, which then resulted in most decisions ensuing from the effect of this tainted, Emotional Tank water. The Emotional Tank simply acts on what has been passed to it from the Cognitive Tank. Cyclical and compounding was its influence, and the more I left it unchecked, the more I accepted it as my normal. When those negative emotions are rationalized and given complete relevance, that's when a treacherous path is set forth, and future struggle is all but assured. With the inviting and, at times, destructive influence of alcohol, this pattern became rote for me in its irrational, self-image-undercutting course. Make a terrible decision, discard the accountability, then repeat as demanded, every time chipping away at the reason why I needed to make the better choice. I was fully aware of this pattern, as I often offered up the solution to others during my years as a counselor, but couldn't quite apply it to my own life. The answer was always there but was increasingly getting buried under my own *pile of crutches*. Do as I say, not as I do. That is a common mantra of about 60 percent of the counselors I know, as most are just as troubled as their clients. I know, I know, making friends wherever I go… At least, I named a good 40 percent! I'll let those counselors place themselves in the group of their choosing! Comfort with discomfort once again ruled the roost, time and time again. Little did I know (or maybe want to know) that there was a better way.

Emotions, when I broke it all down, are truly choices made further up the pipe. I now have realized that those prolonged times of feeling wronged were a choice made out of familiarity and predictability. The urge to resolve issues by rearranging orbital bones in bar parking lots was an easy position to adopt for so many years. Over the last several years, there have been a few individuals who have stress-tested my newfound avenue of conflict resolution via their less-than-admirable behaviors. Redirecting this knee-jerk anger (which is all mine to own) over something I cannot control has been one of the hardest in real time self-trajectory adjustments that I have ever undertaken. Those arrogant and narcissistic actions and words by others have been very valuable in my journey of change, as acceptance and forgiveness have replaced retaliation and feelings of being slighted. Establishing clear and definitive boundaries of what I will not accept was also a crucial step in this process. (Another shout out to Russel Redenbaugh!) I do not judge others in thinking I am better than they are. We are all imperfect beings, but attaining clarity in what I allow into my life has been important in getting to where I've set up camp emotionally. No act of judgment, just exercising the free will to exclude or limit my exposure to those individuals in my life. I just simply have no need for those who place themselves in their self-absorbed tower of delusional importance. Perhaps herein lies the hidden reason for my decision to give up alcohol altogether. Maybe it was a premonition of things to come, as I am pretty sure if I had been engaged in the gate opening of the irrational, the fighter may have been given that driver's seat, which in turn would've resulted in nothing constructive whatsoever. This has been an ongoing process in carving out those new neural pathways and the reconstruction of a better way. Questioning the validity of my own negative emotion producing intellectual narratives has been difficult, yet incredibly empowering. It has definitely proved to be an invaluable gift to self.

As mentioned earlier, depression has the ability to completely bottom out the tap in my tanks, thus giving life to past insecurities and unresolved anger. This was a huge factor in why I wanted something different for myself. In that realization alone, there was a great deal of healing, as I finally stood up for the occupants of my bus. I had enough of feeling out of control in my emotional world, which for many years hinged on external influences rather than internal convictions. Fixing the holes in that internal bucket has lessened the demand and need for outside sources of happiness. Becoming increasingly emotionally settled has taken the pressure off that need to hunt for outer gratification, which in turn has taken away the holding of others' feet to the expectation fire. I have very few expectations in this life other than those I demand from myself. In dealing with my external world, I have replaced expectations with wishes in order to avoid the feeling of disappointment. Sometimes I have to run others' actions through my newfound intellectual filter a few times, but eventually, I get it figured out. I now practice the process of asking myself how much influence the negative actions of others has on my own self-worth. Pretty clear and concise, with the answer increasingly being none whatsoever. If my boat is anchored securely to my own dock, the waves created by others have no lasting effect. I cannot control what others do with their own reckless and ignorant, emotional boating skills. Eventually they will sink their own craft, so no need for me to untie and join the fray. I may even offer them a life jacket in the name of forgiveness. And that dock you attach your vessel to, that would be your cognitive filter made by all that's good in your Spiritual Tank. A new and unfamiliar narrative it was for me, but man, it is legitimately liberating. Awareness that it works, once again, demands action to react accordingly. In the past, when I found those taps plunged to the bottom, I would lose sight of all that is good that is clearly visible when I was above the muck line. For those of you readers who have never felt that vision-limiting darkness, much of this may not make any sense whatsoever. But then again, you probably won't have any reason to read this book, so all is good! Keeping that "this too shall pass" perspective is paramount in taking back the helm and sailing on through the seemingly unending, emotionally destructive fog bank. In the next section, I will describe what gives me that life-saving force that evens everything out during the low swings and allows me to keep my time "below the muck line" to a minimum. That, my book-buying friends, are the blessings flowing out of my Spiritual Tank.

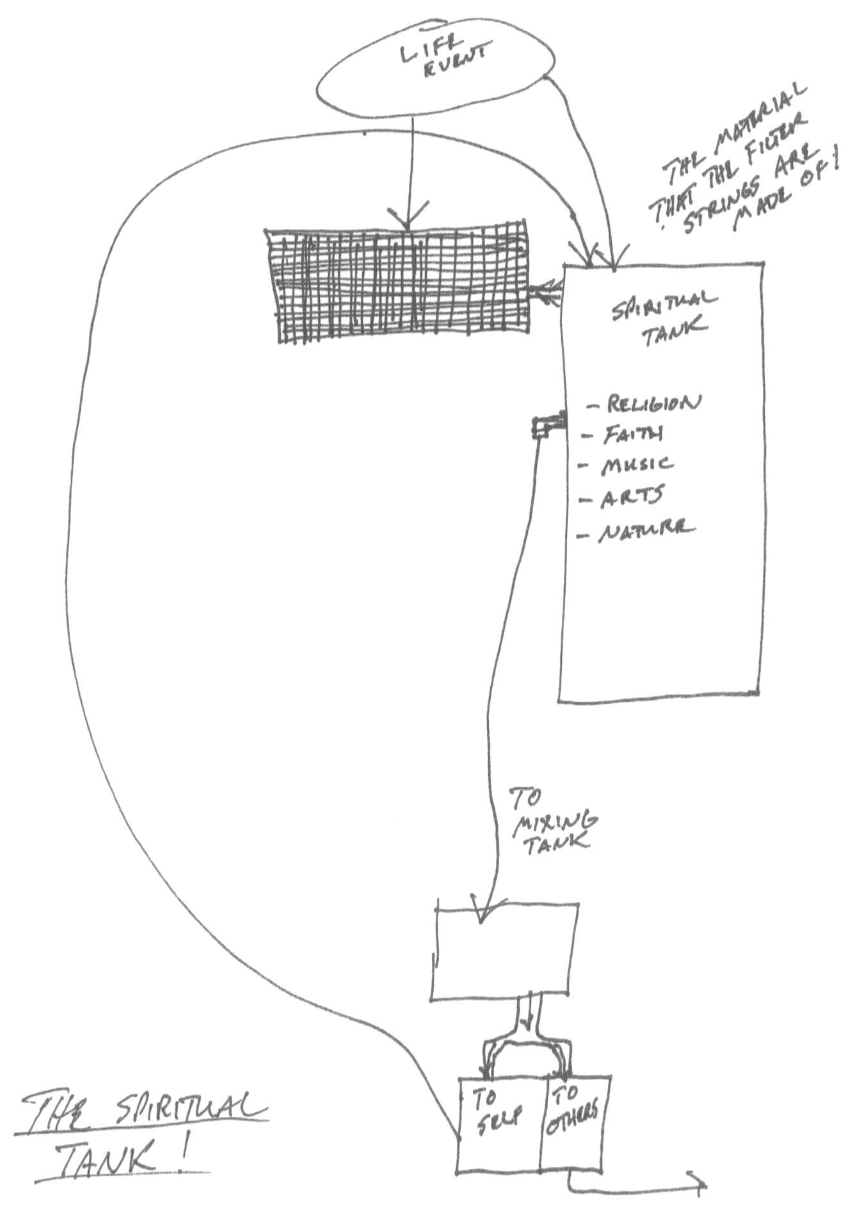

LIFE EVENT
THE MATERIAL THAT THE FILTER STRINGS ARE MADE OF!
SPIRITUAL TANK
- RELIGION
- FAITH
- MUSIC
- ARTS
- NATURE
TO MIXING TANK
TO SELF
TO OTHERS
THE SPIRITUAL TANK!

The Hammer of Faith—the Spiritual Tank

I would venture to bet that a majority of us *Homo sapiens* worship something in our own lives. I have had many conversations with the so-called nonbelievers and have agnostic friends who devoutly believe that science explains all that needs explaining in this universe. I tell them that their religion is science, which means they worship that which is made by man. We then progress into the discussion about heaven. They ask, "If I am a good-hearted person with good moral character but don't believe in God or the existence of final judgment, would I get into your heaven?" I simply reply that if their heart is good, and their morals are solid, they have already been influenced by God, in my opinion. Where one ends up is not for me to judge. I have found that the more devout my faith has become, the fewer answers I have to offer up in regards to "branding others." I suppose that is a byproduct of increased humility. It is a sense of calm that has unseated my need to have all the answers. In my own present-day life, faith represents that life-steadying force that, when fully embraced, can get me through any tragedy in this mortal adventure. True faith is not fleeting, even in the most heartbreaking times and is not something to be used as a token for bartering in rationalizing bad choices. It has emerged as the anchor on the side of my own cliff, providing that spiritual security in that, no matter what happens, I *will* make it through the tribulation. Here in a bit I will give you my own testimony of an experience in 1987 that has repeatedly risen to confirm that my own faith is legitimate and without any doubt or question. Once again, maybe I'm just one of the lucky ones to have had this contact with the Divine.

When I talk about this Spirituality Tank, I am talking about much more than religion. There are many sources in which one can fill that tank with that which represents what is pure, kind, and compassionate. It represents what lies within that moves one to rearrange to the front what is good in the world around them. Religion is just one of those sources, with nature, art, and music also being a few of the "springs for the soul" that give one that undeniable and unwavering sense of serenity. It is from the contents of this tank that the aforementioned cognitive/intellectual filter is molded. It contains the ingredients by which positive intuitions are created and gives us mortals the courage to face each and every day with promise and optimism, no matter what emerges as obstacles on the road ahead. It is herein this tank that, in my opinion, as a society we are failing. We have exchanged what is good for what makes us feel good in the moment. Instead of that peaceful stroll in the middle path, we have recklessly embraced the tumultuous, roaring ride down the hill, all in the name of feeling the thrill, no matter how destructive that crashing ride may be. I myself am first to admit my own choice, time and time again, to veer off onto that tumultuous path that ended in nothing productive, resulting in finding myself lost further down the mountain. In the aforementioned model of the Well Bottom Bar and Grill, my spiritual guy would choose to sit by the door, drinking water, to watch the melee that ensued by the other three entities. Eat, drink, and be merry, for tomorrow, in that hardest bed, I shall lie. So much that is irrational becomes rote when that Spiritual Tank is out of the discussion. I became drawn by the will of the hedonist, which only drove my own existence into a full-blown quest, in the dark, to find answers to questions that I really didn't even have a clue to what the questions were. Talk about being lost. I had silenced the sanest voice of the bunch, all the while clinging to my own shallow and wishful sense of faith. I guess you could say that even though I fully believed in the reality that my crops needed that "spiritual water" to grow, I refused to turn on the head gate to provide the needed water for those crops to thrive. I then would *feel victimized* when my crops suffered. That water lies in wait for all of us. We just have to open up the gates to let it in to replenish and sustain our own fields.

When I finally gave the podium to the spiritual guy, that's when reality finally set in, and the power of unabated faith took back the reins to my own life. The following event is perhaps the most defining experience I have ever encountered. It took years to stick, but today, it is the centerpiece in my own belief in the existence of a Higher Power, which is God and Jesus Christ, my Savior. It was July 7, 1987. It was the day that started out as the end of a much-anticipated course that I mapped out for my life. Little did I know that it actually was only the beginning to a destination that would eventually deliver me to something beyond beautiful and absolutely beyond my own comprehension. They are my *angels on the highway*:

I had it all worked out. Having graduated from Cal State Northridge with a BA in psychology, I had big plans to hire on with LA County Juvenile Probation Department, working as a counselor as Camp Kilpatrick in Malibu, California. I had completed my internship there, and all was going as planned, until there was a hiring freeze in the county. Now on my own, I couldn't afford to live in California anymore, so on to the Trail of Disappointment back home to Colorado I began. With a Chevy Luv pickup with a camper shell and no air-conditioning, I set out on this drive, packed to the gills with all that I owned. With just enough money to get me home on this thirteen-hour drive, I traveled with an overwhelming sense of failure, overlooking my accomplishment of obtaining my second degree in five years, but returning with no real sense of direction. Dressed in only shorts, no shirt, and high-top Converse tennis shoes, I crossed that California-Nevada line at around 11:00 a.m. At Nevada mile marker 7, I noticed a cloud of dust on the right side of the interstate. Rolling to a stop, I saw before me a scene that forever was imbedded in my mind. An older, two-wheel drive Ford pickup was on its side, with a woman lying about ten feet in front of the truck, with a man about fifteen feet from her sprawled face up over the brush. Once stopped, I set the parking brake, leaving the truck running. Being first on the scene, with the dust still settling, I approached the man, who clearly was deceased. I quickly went to my truck and retrieved an old coat that I had managed to keep around through the years and covered him up. Not certain why that was important at the moment, but that was what I did. The woman was barely conscious as I approached her, lying there with an obvious broken left wrist and bloodied from the glass in her face and arms. I then proceeded to lie next to her in the dirt on my left side, holding her and keeping her talking. As more travelers began to stop, one of them was a nurse who was checking the lady for other injuries. Fractured legs, pelvis, and surely internal injuries we couldn't detect. About ten minutes into this horrific situation, the lady asked me about her husband, who when I turned my head, I could see lying there with my coat-covering him. I instructed the others who gathered to get something to hold up between us, which ended up being a sheet someone retrieved, which also helped block the sun on this already 100-degree late morning. As the lady continued to ask about her husband, I could only tell her that he was being attended to. About fifteen minutes into this tragedy, the lady then asked about her baby. A sense of upgraded fear came over all who had assembled. People began looking, but to no avail. Baby things in the truck but no baby. I remember being struck with the horrible thought that the baby may be under the truck. After a little more discussion, she remembered dropping the baby off at her mother's in San Bernardino. A brief moment of relief in this unthinkable tragic scene. This scene carried out for over an hour before the ambulance arrived, with the paramedics picking me up to move me due to my entire left side being numb from the hour ordeal in that position. They then went to work. After getting my feeling back in my left leg, covered in the lady's blood, I returned to my truck, which now had shut down due to the radiator hose springing a leak, losing all water. A traveler gave me two plastic jugs of water, which I added after taping up the hose as best as I could before proceeding to the first rest stop to get more water. I remember the last sight of that scene as I pulled away being that of the deceased man with my old jacket still covering him. Crazy what sticks with us. I repeated this process across the desert, traveling until the water ran out, letting it cool, adding the water from the jugs, then stopping at the next services to fill up the jugs and radiator. I repeated this process across the desert, until sunset fifteen miles west of Beaver, Utah, at which time I had a tire start to come apart. "What more could happen?" is what I remember filling my thoughts…

After hand-cranking the spare tire down from under the truck, I replaced the tire only to have all the water drain out, with no water left in the jugs. My hood wasn't up, and no steam emitting from the engine. Just me with no phone, sitting on the shoulder of the highway, feeling completely defeated, all the while wondering if that lady in the accident had lived. After sitting there for about thirty minutes with no plan, I remember the amazing sunset on the red cliffs across the highway to the north. Once again, crazy what sticks with us. Then it happened. Sitting on the shoulder of the highway, completely drained from the events of perhaps the most trying day of my life, an old, beat-up white hatchback pulled up within four feet of my bumper. The two occupants had big "Woodstock" hair, with the driver being a monster of a being. After they sat there for about two minutes, all I could think was that if they give me a ride to a phone, they can have the truck and all my belongings. I was certain that I was getting rolled. The driver, leaning on the wheel, then proceeded to wave at me as I sat on the shoulder of the highway about twenty-five feet from them. The passenger then proceeded to get out of their rusted out, beat-up rig and retrieved something from the back. With no shirt, no shoes, and odd-looking canvas pants, he approached. I suddenly felt an over whelming sense of peace that to this day, I cannot describe. He moved toward me with hair hanging in his face, blocking all his facial features, then proceeded to set down two jugs of water right next to me, uttering, two feet from my own face, "Need some water, brother?" All I could do was nod yes as I couldn't speak. The aura around me in this moment was nothing I had ever experienced before in my life. From consuming defeat to a complete sense of serenity. He set the jugs down, uttered those words, then returned to the car, after which they drove off, almost as if they just vanished into thin air. As they drove away, I stood to get their license plate number, but there were no plates on this vehicle. I filled the radiator, stopped in Beaver, Utah, to fill the four jugs, then started once again on the quest to get home. I bawled my head off from the beginning of I-70 to Richfield, Utah, completely stunned by this experience. But it wasn't over, just quite yet...

Arriving at Green River, Utah, at around midnight, now seventeen hours into this trip, I had planned to stay the night as I was at the end of my rope, completely exhausted. At that time, there was one gas station at the west end of town, with the water fill station being at the back of the lot. As I filled all the jugs, I heard a rustle in the scrub brush, only to find a hitchhiker standing up to put his pack on. Through the dim lighting from the station, another large man with big hair stood about twenty feet from me down the slight embankment. After a few grunts from his effort to rise to his feet, he looked at me for about ten seconds, then mumbled, "Go home." He then disappeared into the dark, leaving me wide awake and headed home on the remaining last two hours of this life-altering trip.

One would think that the events of that day would have set me on a clear path of resurrected faith. But I went the other way in the coming years, engaging in self-destructive behavior and doomed-to-fail relationships for many years to come. I occasionally would think about that lady, and if she survived, but it wasn't until five years ago on a veterans' fishing trip that this day would come full circle. Sitting on the deck of a fishing boat in a cove in the Haida Gwaii Mountains, I was transported back to that Utah highway. Sitting with United States Army veteran who was battling Huntington's disease, I remember looking at retired SSG David Miller as he sat without any facial twitches for about a minute, eyes closed and a slight smile on his face. In that moment, it was as if I was transported back, feeling the same overwhelming sense of peace that I experienced when I heard those words, "Need some water, brother?" on the side of that Utah highway. I then completely bought in, realizing that all of this is God's work. I remember thinking, *I get it, Lord. I now truly get it…*

In describing the power of this Spiritual Tank in our everyday lives, it is my opinion that some of those that pinpoint religion as their source, at times, do it for the wrong reason. I personally do not attend church, for my main "house of worship" is on that mountain surrounded by all that is not constructed by the hands of man. I know many people who are avid traditional churchgoers that actually do practice what they preach, finding great humility in their quest to live by the doctrines set forth in their religion. But I also find many who use religion as a sword of judgment, building huge "castles of religion" that serve primarily as a means to look down on others while having no door to get into what they have built. I recently heard someone that I have witnessed firsthand engaging in less-than-admirable behavior as part of their own life narrative, state that "I am imperfect. God forgives me, so all is good." I don't believe, for myself, that the path to a better place includes the rejection of making positive changes, then assuming that I get a free pass through those pearly gates just because I think I deserve that pass due to my own self-appointed importance. For many years, I adopted a watered-down version of conviction that bear a rather thin veil of accountability for myself, thus resulting in living with a subconscious false pretense that I can do whatever I wanted, adorning the badge of the forgiven sinner, then continuing on down the road believing that I will be granted access simply due to my sense of mortal enti-tlement. Arrogance leads to ignorance, and the tornado continues on its destructive path. I now have embedded that, yes, I do make mistakes, which can be forgiven, but the soulful dedication to change is binding in my search for redemption and forgiveness. Being a good Christian is extremely difficult at times, hence the belief that any-thing that carries great value comes with the requirement of hard work and sacrifice. Talent alone (having the ability to say I believe) is not enough, as it also takes effort, conviction, and devotion (liv-ing out what I believe). That is probably the most meaningful rev-elation that I have found in my search to keep my Spiritual Tank flowing, without reservation, in my own life. Being a good Christian and adopting all values of such is a high and hard road to travel, but the reward is truly a reconciling force for the soul. In this ongoing dance with depression, faith has given me that internal anchor that reverberates that all will be okay and keeps the good stuff in my tanks within view during those low times. Beautiful, crushing, spiritual humility. I would be in a much worse spot in my life without it. Perhaps, not even here at all.

Side Bar—Dancing with the Ghost

As I mentioned before, those who have never felt the life-limit-ing weight of depression probably will never understand much in this project. Until you have found yourself in that dance with the unseen, a dance that pushes one to the darkest, deepest depths of one's tank, most of what I'm writing about may not make much sense. But that's okay, and God bless you for not having to deal with such a restricting force. Hopefully, this account sheds some understanding of the condition. For those who are fully engaged with this smothering waltz, perhaps the same may ensue, which is, a better understanding. In sharing my experiences, it is easy to formulate a presentation due to the fact that it is not something I have to imagine, something I've learned, or a theory I've formulated from observation of others, but is something that I have lived with for most of my life.

Depression is a part of my being, and I now have exposed it in all of its negative glory. No more letting it run amok in the darkness and letting it take the destructive lead in the dance of my life. Many do not take the time to dissect why they feel the way they do, many times due to the fear of what they might find and the change in narrative that it will demand for any correction in their dance routine to occur. I still dance with that ghost from time to time, but I do not let it lead me. The dance that depression leads is one that has no defined steps at all, but simply it stops the dance, dragging the helpless to the darkest corner of the ballroom. It is from there where the affected watch as the interpreted paralyzing grip of "the ghost" holds one hostage as everyday life and its responsibilities continue in its dance on the floor in the distance. With every *missed song*, self-guilt rises to further increase the feeling of helplessness. Knowing you have to get back out there, but irrationally giving way the demands of the ghost to stay locked in a posture of immobility. It becomes dire when the ghost leads one completely out of the light and out of sight of the good in one's life, even though ever-so-present. I have been "around that corner," and for much of my life, I self-medicated to the point that I was allowed to stagger back onto the dance floor only to create havoc that drew me back even further into the grip of depression due to the shame that ensued. The ghost is patient and knows that you will return after the train wreck due to the need to hide in the darkness to avoid that light cast upon the fresh round of self-induced shame. You see, the endgame for the ghost is to alienate, to isolate, and to destroy, and too often is successful when left unchecked. Tragically, the only option for way too many is to quit dancing altogether, thus ending in the taking of one's own life. This was where I found myself seventeen years ago, and since have emboldened myself to never leave the floor ever again. Do I still find myself having to dance with that really shitty dance partner from time to time? Absolutely. It is in my conviction to take back that control in those times that keep me dancing. I don't always get to choose who I have to dance with, but I do choose where I tolerate this potentially suffocating "no step" partner. It can be done, for I have done it. You just have to decide that you are worth the fight.

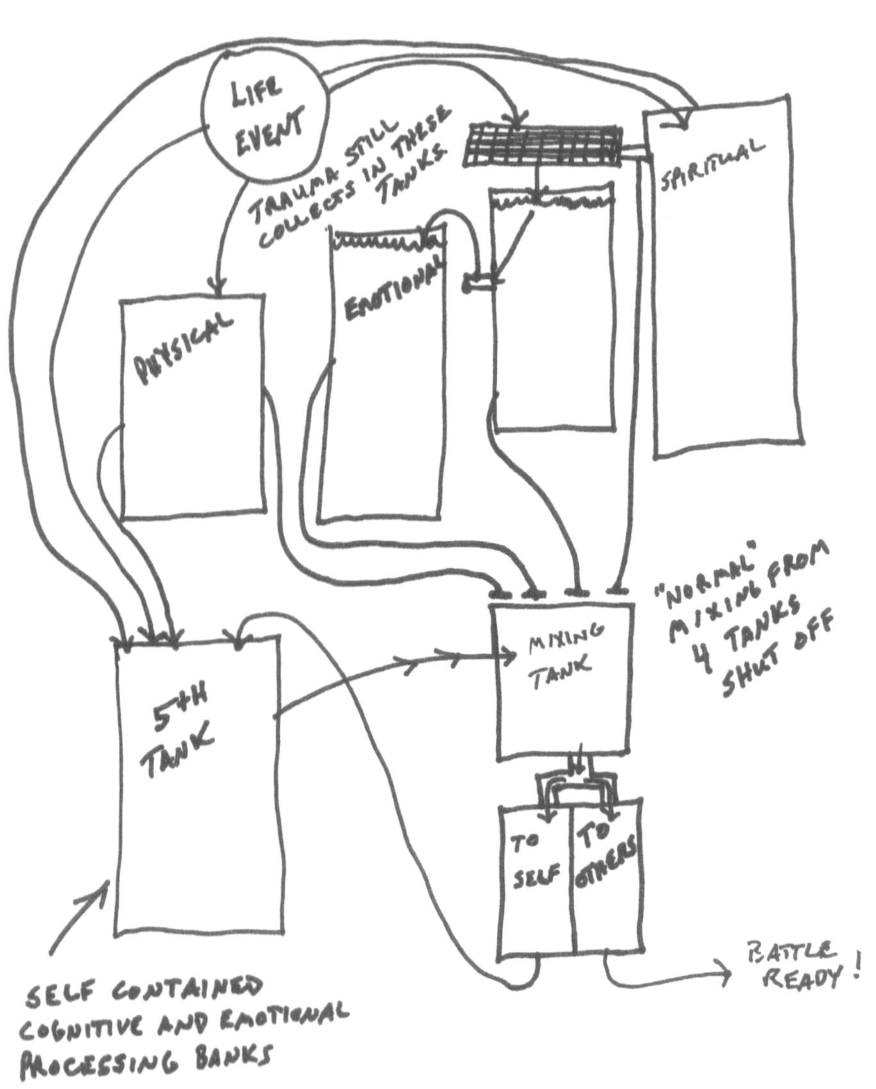

LIFE EVENT
TRAUMA STILL COLLECTS IN THESE TANKS
SPIRITUAL
PHYSICAL
EMOTIONAL
5TH TANK
MIXING TANK
"NORMAL" MIXING FROM 4 TANKS SHUT OFF
TO SELF
TO OTHERS
BATTLE READY !
SELF CONTAINED COGNITIVE AND EMOTIONAL PROCESSING BANKS
THE 5TH TANK !

The Fifth Tank

Now that my ADD has produced a stray from the layout, allow me to present my observation to what I refer to as the Fifth Tank. In meeting and coming to truly love many Veterans and Gold Star Family members over the last ten years, this observation found me. As I mentioned before, I never served, so in talking about veterans' issues I am full of it and do not know what I'm talking about. The Fifth Tank is simply my observation in describing what *may* occur with *some* veterans once they are out and called on to reconstruct life as a civilian. The content of this tank, in my opinion, is the most pure and addictive, mortal fluid in the world, which is dedication to one's brothers and sisters in the face of death. Many first responders may also develop this tank in their own lives. It is self-contained with its own cognitive processing center as well as its separate emotion management compartment. Out of this tank, unbreakable bonds are formed that stay with those who have served, especially in combat, for the rest of their lives. Those relationships become the most cherished, thus amplifying the resulting, crushing loss when a team member is lost in combat, to duty, or to suicide. In talking with many who have served multiple combat deployments, this tank plays an even more crucial role. All the traumatic experiences that one may be faced with in combat, in my opinion, ends up in the other four respective tanks, with this Fifth Tank being mainlined at times, simply as a means to bold survival. I've heard many describe the incredible draw of wanting to get back to their unit while in between deployments. For many, the other four tanks may be full of "war muck" due to the trauma of battle, so the more reason to mainline the power of the Fifth Tank. Their new normal has been recreated, and the definition of what is normally desired has shifted. It is when these warfighters finally get out for good that the potential for struggle raises its ugly head. The Fifth Tank is turned off, and the veteran is now left to deal with the mire in the other tanks that has mounted over the months, or even years, unchecked, unaddressed, and unfiltered. It is the transitioning of the controls back to the "conventional water treatment system," a system that has possibly in some cases, not been used in years. Those whose tanks that are full of trauma often find their taps clogged with nothing coming out. Call it a form of withdrawal, if you will, but the absence of that "razor's edge" everyday life can leave a monstrous void, if left unaddressed.

Enter the self-medication phase, which entails the *mixing in* of self-destructive behavior fluid just to get *something* to flow. When that trauma at the bottom is blended with the good stuff at the top (and yes, there is always some good at the top), that is when the ensuing output becomes unrecognizable, and the struggle catches another gear. Clarity is lost, and the urge to further self-medicate continues to ramp up in its destructive cycle. Comfort with discomfort becomes the new norm simply because it becomes predictable. "You have changed" or "You seem like a different person." I suspect some vets have heard from friends and loved ones after discharge from the service. Of course, they may seem different, for they have been operating in a totally different life-evaluating system that is foreign to us civilians. This is not abnormal or bad in itself, just as trying to sync a MacBook with a Macintosh is abnormal or bad. It's just that, when they get out, they are working in between two completely different operating systems during this reintegration. Throughout this difficult search for the guide to transition back to that so called "normal civilian laptop" (whatever the hell *normal* might mean), that Fifth Tank remains intact and untapped, even though it may be perceived, by some, to have been lost forever. Maybe not so much missing the brutality of the actual battlefield, but more so missing the first-level connection and dedication to those who battled beside them. I can't even imagine how consuming this search must be for those that find themselves in the "after fight," for I, myself, cannot even begin to relate. The fortitude and resilience of those Veterans is an awe-inspiring testament to the power of the human spirit.

Now that I've *uneducatedly* (yes, a new word, according to the "Spellcheck Red Underlining Pen Wizard behind the screen) described my observation of the scene, what about the remedy or corrective action? My answer is I don't really know for sure, as this answer is elusive at best. But my response/ uneducated guess is this. First, in my opinion, the "mixing" or self-destructive behavior must stop before anything changes. Call it the resurrection of the baseline or the sober view of the contents of one's tank. Clarity of what lies in the bottom however ugly it may be and clarity of where ones "muck line" starts in the other tanks are the prerequisite for any lasting change or understanding to begin to take root. Add in any physical injuries into this mix and a powerful runaway train is all set for the throttle to be engaged. It will probably be a most difficult task for most, as it requires a restart of the intellectual filter (next chapter), and the abandonment of the narratives and mindset that probably kept them alive while in combat. Trauma stays in all of our tanks, with the goal being the education of oneself on how to keep that tap above, or at least near the muck line in those episodes of crushing anxiety and confusion. So much tragedy in this fight for clarity, not only in the veterans' community, but in the general population as well. After this first part is addressed, then comes the even more difficult task of understanding the true composition of your own water.

Finding a way to tap back into this Fifth Tank has proven to help in this transition for many vets, as witnessed firsthand via the veterans' program I founded with Scott Brown in 2011, Base Camp 40, Warriors in the Wild. This is the underlying purpose of all veterans' programs, in my opinion. Many veterans have "replumbed" their lines, so to speak, to tap back into their Fifth Tank via the connection established to their other four. It is in that BC40 Tank where the materials are found that they use in their own "repiping" project. Not as pure, but the Fifth Tank fluid is still there to empower and strengthen their lives here at home, for the "good lions" lie in wait in that Fifth Tank to be embraced. Connecting with other veterans is undoubtedly the most important door that we open with these outdoor adventures. This expands their safety net around them and increases their awareness that they are not alone in this fight. Opening that door to that *gift of the wild* also allows for one to let their tanks settle for a few days, all the while adding some really clean water at the top. In the end, the veterans do the work and deserve 100 percent of the credit for the resets that they may encounter. I know it has humbled me in ways I have yet to realize, and I thank the

Lord for giving me the vision to create such a model and vision that is now shared and enhanced by many in this organization. Another future literary project will be an in-depth look at this mission to give back. The Hammer of Giving will be another adventure, for sure, as the road of generosity is not as smooth as one might think.

Further expounding upon the topic of the unknown for me, the impact of PTS (post-traumatic stress) and TBI (traumatic brain injury) makes this process of obtaining the aforementioned clarity that much more difficult. My past experiences have surely set the stage for some PTS, but there is a monstrous difference in my experiences in comparison to that of veterans and first responders. I was not dodging bullets, mortars, fearing IEDs, or the loss of my own life or that of some of my closest friends in those moments. I understand the dynamics of PTS, but when it comes to veterans and first responders, you could say I recognize the book, but will never know what's in it. Adding a strong dose of survivor guilt also increases the burden on this journey for many. I wrote this awhile back after a deep discussion with a veteran, reflecting on what he had said about this topic:

The Reason It Wasn't Me

Fallin' into that darkest place, I feel it comin' on,
Memories, they charge on in, of the ones that now are gone,
I teeter on the edge of the fall, into this blinding well,
Sometimes I wanna let go of it all, but my story, I've yet to tell.

When I seek the reason, it wasn't me, it's an answer never found,
At least not in an outer sense, for that answer has no sound.
I've chased that question, to depths untold,
but end up without relief.
I've broken the lock, then walked away, like an empty-handed thief.

A million times and a million tears, the response is all the same.
I'll gut the room and hammer and thrash,
but no one's there to blame.

How long do I chase? How deep do I
plunge, to find one without a face?
I just wish I could start anew, and these thoughts, I would erase.

But there looms a mountain I must climb, to give it all to God.
Anything else is a spiritual crime, within my soul, it's induced fraud.
The reason why it wasn't me, is simply *He* called for them.
I now must fight on through the fire, to live life for those friends.

Personally, I do not use the *D* or disorder at the end of PTS, as post-traumatic stress is a natural reaction to an abnormal event. If you break your leg, you have an injury to your leg, not a leg disorder. The same applies to your psyche, injured due to the painful impact of traumatic experiences that find themselves wreaking havoc on the Intellectual, Emotional, and Spiritual Tanks. I think that using the description of this being a disorder may, in some cases, bring a life-defining, control-limiting stigma to this fight, similar to my view on depression. In no way am I minimizing in any way, shape, or form the reality and potentially crushing impact of PTS. Here is a metaphor that found me the other day while loading a coal train for four hours:

"Post-traumatic stress is like the inflatable pontoons that are attached to traumatic experiences. The old saying of "Birds of a feather, flock together" holds true with PTS. Let's say you have plenty of trauma in the bottom of your tank, but you have gained some clarity of what lurks beneath the surface of the muck. You find yourself tapped above the muck line and doing pretty good. Well, along comes a triggering event, baring similar fangs of one of those monsters of the deep. This is where the awareness of what's at the bottom of your tank finds its purpose. If you know what's there, you can then identify what's connected to the pontoons that are rushing to the surface. So here comes the trigger and the pontoons are then deployed, as the monster rises to the top to greet its "shit bird partner in torment." The choice in that moment is crucial, as the draw to self-medicate may present itself, causing another round of shit-stirring. One can also hold the tap point and *pull the plug* on those pontoons to allow both to return to their rightful place in the bottom of their tank. Clarity and faith can be helpful tools in the deflation process. Hold the ground and ride it out. An extremely romantic and simplistic view of this dynamic but a different view all the same.

In my own life, I experienced a traumatic incident (small when compared to that of others I know) that involved a man taking his own life on the tracks in front of our train sixteen years ago. A gruesome scene it was, and in the ensuing days, I experienced a jolt of anxiety that fortunately for clarity, I was able to connect the dots. Two days after the incident, I pulled a gray stocking cap out of the pocket of my old ranch coat, which resembled that of what the man was wearing. Due to the onboard debriefing I did with the conductor right there on the engine, I was able to identify the source of the anxiety and let it float on down to the bottom. I never lost a night of sleep over this scattering of body parts, which I directly attribute to my critical incident stress debriefing training. Everything in our immediate environment was now attached to that event, so cataloging those items was crucial for my own "down the road resource for control." Once again, knowing what lies at the bottom is pretty important in this pontoon management process. Many never take the time to identify the potential threats that lie within, then simply accept their own emotional roller coaster as their new normal. At times, we create our own domes of happiness and relent to this new restriction on our lives. In the BC40 program, I call our events "hole-puncher trips," not in the sense of checking off a bucket list item, but in the context of punching a hole through that self-constructed, limiting dome. Just being able to get a small breath of that next level air of inner peace is all one needs. That, my friends, is called hope and faith. Just knowing that it exists is 51 percent of the battle. I had a veteran call me after one of the British Columbia fishing trips, asking me, "What happened to me on that boat?" I just told him. "You found it," referring to that new air above his previously accepted, shackling dome of anxiety. He did the work and relished in that newfound atmosphere of hope. Much work to be done as it is an ongoing process but just finding that bit of clarity drastically changed his trajectory.

The aforementioned incident with PTS is a small example of my own experience. Another possible, not-so-troubling holdover from the incident described in the Spiritual Tank is my knack for having a number of extra coats in the back seat of my truck. I never gave it much thought until about a year ago when I was doing my biannual clean out of my "survival capsule," known as my vehicle, when it dawned on me that I have clung to that subconscious need for extra jackets. An a-ha moment it was. I guess I just never know when one of them may needed. Once again, crazy what is retained from traumatic experiences of the past.

In summation of this Fifth Tank, I can only hope that some-one may "find another seat in the stadium" to view this potentially nonsensical Fifth Tank model, maybe shedding a small sliver of light on their management of their own PTS. Life is not about being free of troubling issues. It's a big world that is full of challenges that can jump out at any moment to summon the harsh events of the past. I also have used the metaphor of the wounded lion in the dark. Trauma injects that wounded lion into our house, and it is there for-ever. Engaging in self-destructive, self-medicating behavior is equiv-alent to turning out the lights, thus leaving that wounded lion to stage its attack. Wounded lions hunt at night, thus the importance of keeping the lights on in order to retain any sense of control in those, at times, feeling out-of-control moments. Those good, valorous lions still exist to protect, all which are found in that Fifth Tank. Draw on their courage and strength to get you through the hardest times when one of those wounded lions has you by the throat and is dragging you down into the basement where, sadly, that staggering, blind suffering lies in wait. It's not about getting those wicked hunters out of your life, for they will reside there forever. It's purely about damage con-trol, self-preservation, and gaining the skills of being able to manage all your lions.

God bless all who wage this fight and never forget that you are never completely stuck. Reach out to see the light of another day and embrace that inner voice that tells you that you are worth the fight, no matter how faint that voice may be.

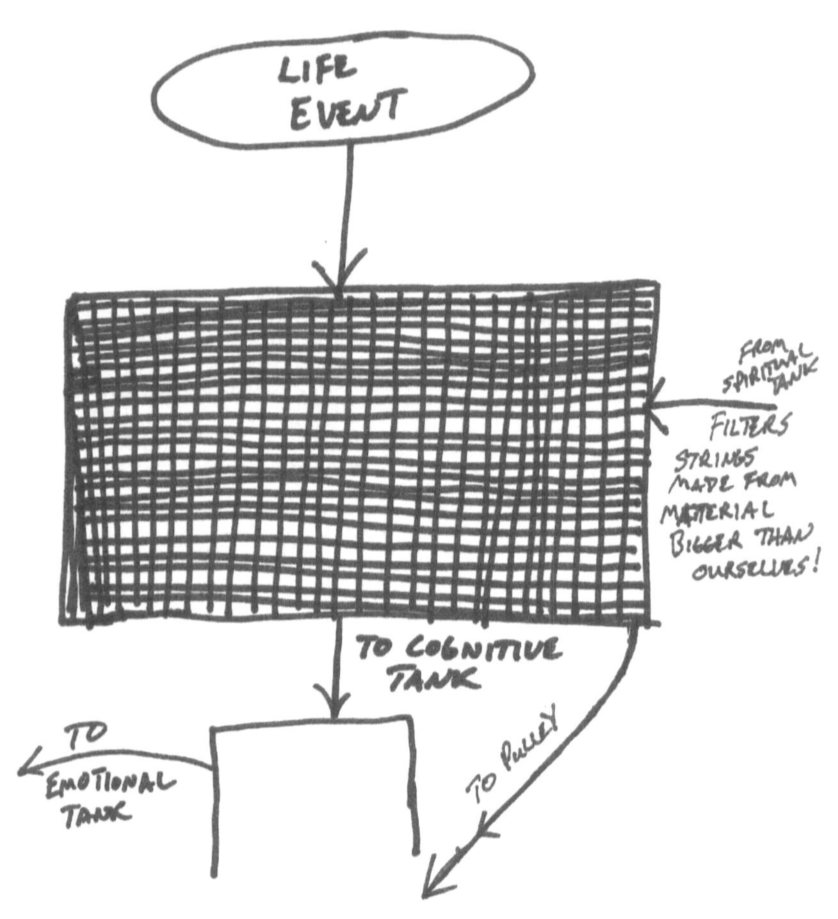

- WHEN SPIRITUAL TANK IS LIMITED, MATERIAL FROM THE COGNITIVE TANK IS USED TO CONSTRUCT THE STRINGS.

THE COGNITIVE/INTELLECTUAL FILTER!

The Million-Dollar Horse in this Race— the Cognitive/Intellectual Filter

We walk through this life with our own interpretation book of external events that influence the direction of our lives. How many of us ever question the construction of this manual that filters all that is presented before us? In the construction of this tank model, the importance of this "interpretation book" or "cognitive/ intellectual filter" found its relevance and definition as the anchor point of all that is processed. It is the writer of my life script and the director of my, at times, run-amok play. The fiber of the strings that make up my own filter is the entwinement of my moral convictions, life narratives, spiritual devotions, and my value of love, forgiveness, and acceptance of self. It is here where the character and value of that incoming water is labeled and designated, with the input/event retaining the residue of the filter itself. My filter has been ever-changing, going from a seine comprised of guilt, shame, and wavering self-worth to one of grace, acceptance, kindness, compassion, and devout acceptance. It is far from perfection, but it is what allows me to limit my errors in judgment and allows me to unload the burdens carried from days of yore. It is the answer to the question of "Who am I?" asked of the one in the mirror. For many years, I glided through this life with no clear understanding of that question, relying on the events of every new day to define who I was. A roller coaster of a life it has been, and the pressure of temporary pleasure-seeking was given full reign. The filter at that time was one of disappointment and failure, which consequently gave rise to the need to please and the external locus of control. Throw in the cloak of depression into this process, and man, what a mess! Through those years, I still had good stuff coming in, but the reward often went unused due to the placement of my tap in the bottom half of my tanks. And yes, the good water is forever in your tanks as well. Constructing that new internal locus of control, or "good filter" has allowed me to, more often, stay tapped above that muck line to thrive on the good water of my past and present and has limited the impact of the "dirty water" dumped in by the external world.

Keeping those filter strings tight and right is an ongoing process but what a revelation and indescribable asset it has been.

Every one of us has a different set of strings in our respective intellectual filters, constructed by our own individual narratives. Traumatic events have a huge impact on those strings, often breaking some, or even all of them, by the weight of its unexpected crash into our tanks. It is in the fallout of traumatic events where the impact forms its legacy. The broken strings are either replaced with forgiveness, faith, and love, restrung with the barbed wire of anger, rage, and soul-consuming sorrow, or never replaced at all. Those are all-natural responses to the hard stuff in our lives, and those things reside in our tanks to, over time, be painfully processed or be terminally given the crown to the kingdom. For the Gold Star fathers and family members I have met over the last nine years, this is what I see that defines their road to living with the loss of their loved one. My heart truly heaves for those men and women, where once again, I cannot begin to relate. Yes, I have experienced the loss of a father but have never felt the crushing loss of a child. Losing an elderly parent is hard, but is something that looms for all of us. Laying to rest a child is not in the script, so there is no chance to prep. Their strength is something I can only revel at, and to say this process is heart-wrenching is definitely an understatement.

It is this filter that defines us after loss and grief, as everything following is influenced by its composition. Simply put, the impact of trauma is twofold. One, it damages the strings of our filters, and two, it completely contaminates the water in our tanks. Repairing that filter, in my opinion, is the starting point in that dance with crushing trauma. The lifelong process of filtering and search for what I call "bitter harmony" with life-altering events is perpetual. A traumatic event never truly sheds its horns. We simply get stronger, become more skilled in moving like a matador, and learn to live with the heavy in our tanks. The composition and maintenance of those strings determine our lane of travel in everyday life, and is a task that some, understandably, fail to address.

There are many inspirational quotes that remind us of the good in life, but how often does it stick beyond ten minutes after reading it? Yes, we allow it to flow into our tanks. We feel good about its meaning, but an hour later find ourselves right back in the same emotional dilemma. It is in the filter where lasting, interpretive change is constructed, and the headwaters of that struggle is addressed. As mentioned before (many times!), I believe that every emotion gets its start in an intellectual narrative, which is where interpretations of events get their marching orders. When I changed out/ reconstructed my filter with strings of forgiveness and accountability, most (not all, I would add) of my emotional "cage wars" subsided. When tainted, external water is presented, my first level of filtering is, "Can I control it?" If the answer is no, then the gravitational value of that water is lightened; it's given a value of acceptance and forgiveness, then sent on into the intellectual tank to be processed. Without that positive filtering, negative actions of others are given a free pass into the intellectual tank, quickly passed to the Emotional Tank, and it is there where the wrestling match begins. Sometimes I have to run it through a few times to get it worked out due to hold over of "old filter strings," but at least, I now have the clarity to know the difference.

It is in this filter where accountability and responsibility for every reaction to life events is found, no matter what others may say or do. When my filter was tainted, so went my interpretation of the world around me. We all make judgment calls on the value of others actions, which in the past I carried over to judging them as a person. Enter stage right my rediscovered faith, which ultimately relinquished character judgment to a task left to someone with a higher pay grade, that being the good Lord. I also no longer give out "remotes" to others to determine my happiness, as my happiness is for me to define through the awareness derived from this newfound filter. We all seek that sense of "needing to be in control" of our lives, and when my filter was a little shady, at best, the need to control my external world became the focus. It's like I had gaping holes in my roof and constantly had to buy new furniture due to the rain destroying the contents of my house. I would then go outside to try and control the approaching storms, cursing the clouds, and laying fault with the rain. Every time I stepped outside to rant at the sky, it tended to rain just a little harder. Through this filter, I fixed my roof, for that is all I truly control. Once the roof was fixed, the soaking impact of the rain was removed, thus resulting in my energy being directed at designing the feng shui of my own abode. I see so many (yes, I was once one of them) trying to control others' actions and the external world around them, which basically is a desperate need for some sense of inner control that they severely lack. Big hearts, but unfortunately a bigger, starving ego that demands the controls in their futile search for inner peace. An exhausting task this was for me, I can tell you. The exhaustion from this dizzying merry go round was surely one of the motivations behind this project. I simply stepped off, for engaging in such fruitless and compounding negative action is a choice we all have the option to make. It just took me awhile to give up that self-constructed throne in my own flimsy tower of self-worth. Meaningful change in perspective is more so grounding than it is uplifting. Eliminate the danger of the flimsy towers, and it is the stability of solid ground you will find.

As I mentioned in an earlier chapter, the tightness of my "filter strings" is directly influenced by the position of my tap on my Intellectual Tank. Yes, I have changed out the strings, but depression clearly influences the tightness of those strings via the pulley mechanism also described earlier in this book. Awareness of this effect has been crucial in limiting the defining power of those low times, for now I swing that pulley over to my Spiritual Tank to keep those strings taunt. Eventually, my goal is to "tie off" the filter from outside influence, embracing the material in my Spiritual Tank to construct, repair, and improve in this ongoing process to define who I am and who I want to be. Much more complex than what I lay out in this book, I know, but it has given me a valid base to build that road map to a better way. Breaking the intellectual/emotional habit of doing what is familiar is really, really trying, but it all started with having the courage to reexamine what really is important and what is looking back at me in the mirror. In my filter, I have changed my own life priorities by "not only putting God back into my own classroom, but putting God at the front of my class to instruct." I also removed concern for what others think of me in the construction of my purpose on this earth. If I infuse all that is good into what I can control,

I then take care of business on the front end, not leaving it up others to rate my performance. You never know when others may or may not have a biased judge in one of their chairs. It does not mean that I do not value the feedback of others, but it's just that I don't let it define my course of action. If my filter is sound, I will know before anyone else if I have made a mistake and will make amends without being directed to do so. There are those out there that will load up on irrational self-guilt just because someone was offended, then send it into the subconscious "I did nothing wrong but will feel responsible anyway" file. This file holds the irreconcilable self-guilt that eventually will overflow and burst at the seams. Definitely, a setup of one-self, for sure. Self-monitoring will tell me when I need to make that correction and can easily do so because of this renewed stability of my own footing found in my more positive life perspective.

Lacing that filter with humility also makes this process an easy one to manage, for we all at some point and time will create some tainted water that we put out to others. Catch it, correct it, and move on. We give that same water back to ourselves, so if our filters are honed, we will know it when it happens. I know those who evade self-corrections due to their "all-or-nothing" filter composition, for being wrong cracks that door to all that lies in the "I *am* wrong" closet of their poor self-image. In making those amends, I cannot control others' ability to forgive, so after the correction, my work is done, and I forge on, not lying in wait for something that may not ever present itself. And if they don't forgive, well, that is their choice. I don't make amends to receive forgiveness, but do it as a means to put closure on a wrongdoing. If they choose to hang onto the incident, that is their way of coping. Be prepared, as many will hold onto such wrongdoings, using it as a hammer when all other tools are lost. That "when in doubt, just use a hammer" concept applies to more than just fixing all things mechanical. I know this because I was a master carpenter in this hammer-wielding in my own past failed "I dos." That past, twisted knack for saving old hammers, I must clearly own. I'm sure those three ex-wives will surely agree with me on this one.

A really important revelation occurred right as I was finishing this book, a revelation regarding the material used to construct the strings of our filters. When my Spiritual Tank was not fully acknowledged, my fallback was to construct those strings with material from my own tainted Cognitive/ Intellectual Tank. This often resulted in a filter-tainted by my own past and of what resided in the bottom of the unresolved. This led to classic cases of projection, which more or less means, I interpreted external events by subconsciously linking them to my own past misdeeds. This subconscious filtering served up the old "that's why I did it, so that means that's why they are doing it" train of thought. This is probably the most commonly practiced, destructive string construction/ event interpretation in society today. I know I was once a third-degree black belt in this sport of "judgment judo" as my convictions were almost solely created by my own experiences. This throws in a whole new level of conflict when you have two parties sparring with this same type of dysfunction. I unfortunately had found my past infiltrated by a world of my own past deeds. I believe this is the meaning of the, at times, accurate saying, "What we most dislike in others is what we most dislike about ourselves." If we are engaging with others with similar shortcomings, our interpretation may be correct, but our classification carries more weight than it should due to it being loaded down with our own insecurities. The gap presents itself in cases where the others' meaning or intent is different than our own interpretation. Now you have the beginning of a possible irreconcilable difference. You see, I believe that those strings need to be woven by material bigger than ourselves, thus the importance of having a fully functioning, healthy Spiritual Tank. Once I found that "divine material," the process of changing my narrative to one of positivity became a much clearer task. I have discovered the clarity of what my filter used to be constructed within those years of struggle. Guilt bred suspicion, resentment of the self leads to lack of trust in others, and unresolved shame encouraged easily reached rage. I often felt trapped within my own constructed walls and blamed others for my predicament. I guess when you have no working tools in your toolbox, desperation for solutions lead to irrational attempts to fix what is broken. I got so used to this narrative as it existed without question and was allowed to taint my tanks without correction. Our intellectual narratives represent that command center by which all is controlled. Having to "come back home" to the devout belief that God's plan is bigger than any itinerary I could construct was that point of no return back into that permanent sense of defeat. With that acceptance of the role that faith plays in creating that filter, the pressure was lifted, thus opening up that portal to soul-liberating forgiveness. Repetitive I may be in much of this book, but I cannot possibly overemphasize this gift of the road map to that quiet and calm that's now found in my present-day existence. So much more out there to discover, cementing that belief that education in any sense simply exposes myself to an even greater world of what I do not know. Accurate is this statement in regards to my purpose in this life. Definitely, so much out there to find in this search for everlasting joy.

I now live by the belief that I am never stuck, at times just temporarily lacking the correct option. This is what this revamped filter has uncovered. By definition and by any standard of conduct, another's actions may be wrong, but my reaction and response to that behavior is mine to own and mine to articulate. Reworked boundaries, forgiveness, accountability, and clarity of the impact of choices I make has been a savior in this revamping of how I respond to situations, situations that my old filter would have demanded swift, emotionally draining action. Kicking that negativity can down the road was a skill perfected at one time in my life. But it's been work, a lot of work I would add, in finding the road map to that middle lane of serenity and resolution. Finding that gift of being able to step out of old mindsets has been a blessing and is something that I hope to convey in this project. Be brave, be willing, and be steadfast in your own search. You and you alone hold the map to discovering your own better way.

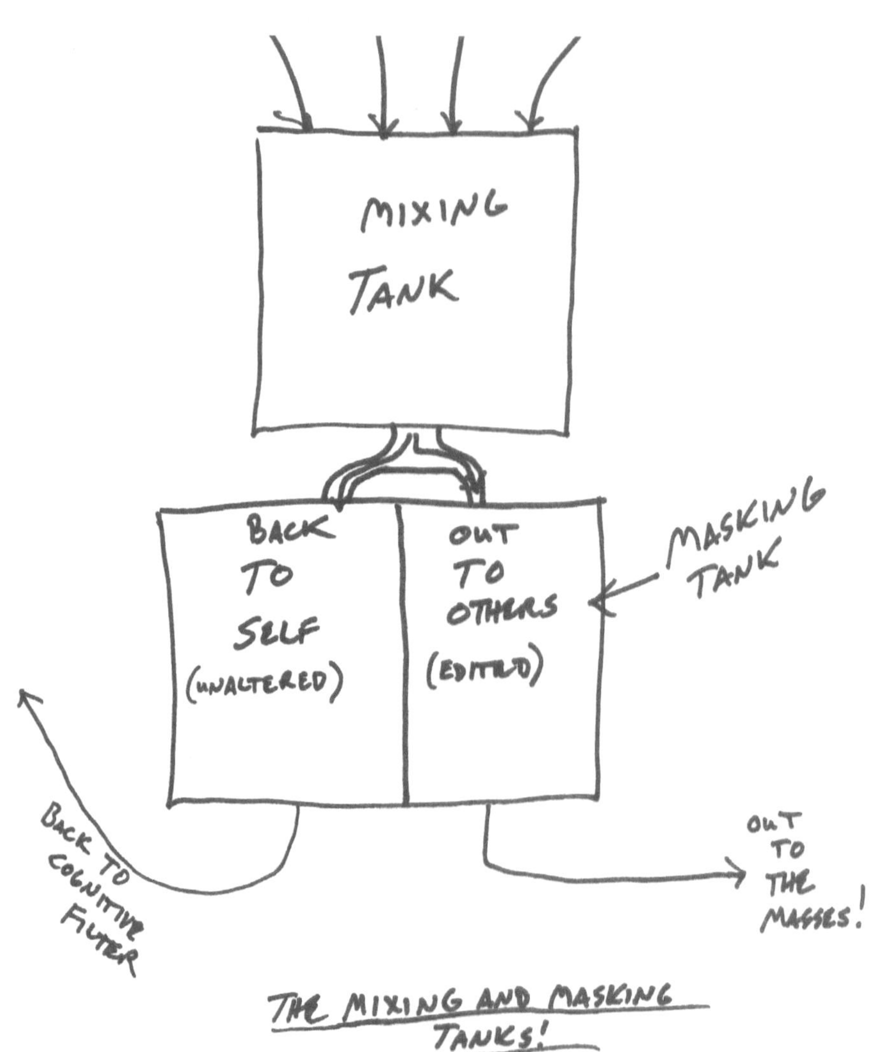

MIXING TANK
BACK TO SELF (UNALTERED)
OUT TO OTHERS (EDITED)
MASKING TANK
BACK TO COGNITIVE FILTER
OUT TO THE MASSES!
THE MIXING AND MASKING TANKS!

The Masking Phase/Process and the Final Edit

Earlier I had mentioned how I used to mask or hide the troubles within, with my personal go-to cover being humor. The tub where all the output of the four tanks is collected for distribution to others and recycled back to myself is split into two compartments. The final product that is presented to the world often went through the masking process prior to its release. You often hear others in their description of someone that was presumably even-natured that commits a terrible act, say something like "He seemed so nice" or "I had no idea." The facade of "all is well" is what I constructed in this final phase, giving others a misleading appearance of what was really rumbling in my war room. While this process took place, the unaltered version was recycled back to my negativity-laced intellectual filter, continuing the cycle of struggle. This masking process actually, in a way, had its positives, as it was carried out by the concern for how others viewed me. When I was "in the well," clinging to that concern was much better than having no regard for my self-image. We all could probably rein in our judgment of others as we just never know what troubles others are trying to mask in their own water. Looking back, I think I subconsciously "bet the farm" on the high level of skill my maskers possessed. This led to making changes up the pipeline that much less important. Losing that concern for what was dispersed is when my inner masking was replaced by outer crisis, and the "out of control" was exposed. I clearly recall having that tipping point during my own "drunken dives into the tank." Those manning my *masking booth* found themselves passed out on the floor, and all sense of the rationality was lost, leaving the tainted water free to flow to others. In writing this book, I have uncovered just how troubled I was in those earlier years. Drink to cover the strife, proceed to go over the line of just being buzzed, then end the night with a whole lot more regret, shame, and disappointment than I had started with. The avalanche continued down the hill, getting stronger the farther down the mountain it traveled. Sometimes we just get tired of the process, and let it all out to create more compounding shame. A good read on this exact topic is the book *Shame and Addiction* by the aforementioned author John Bradshaw. Really good stuff in that book that addresses this process. Do I consider my behavior shameful, or do I see myself as shameful? A big difference between the two as behaviors aren't as impactful as narratives. The first is a symptom, while the second is the cause. By addressing the cause and eliminating the need for that alteration of the real, I have almost completely removed the importance of the maskers. The water is good to go without the constant need to "pretty it up" prior to its dispersal to the world. I have dealt with it further up the pipelines of this complex "water plant," leaving those maskers with little to do. What a crazy cycle I had embraced and, like I said before, just feeling blessed and lucky to be alive.

CHAPTER 6

The Ying-Yang Shuffle

Okay, earlier in this book, I did state that I would address the issue of relationships in a later chapter. Now that it's a later chapter, here goes a whole lot of what not to do! Having an extensive and thorough résumé of failed relationships and marriages, I feel I can confidently comment on this shuffling dance between the yin and yang. There are hordes of books out there on this topic of how to repair the dance steps of two people who struggle with the awareness of what their own dance means to themselves, let alone what it means in reference to their relationships with others. You will often hear from counselors and read in self-help books about the value of forgiveness and compromise in restoring and maintaining harmony in this at times "race to 'til death do us part." A thought-provoking reading in this field of matrimony can be found in what's called Occam's razor, a writing of the fourteenth-century scholastic philosopher and theologian, William of Ockham. Mr. Ockham more or less stated that "All things being equal, the simplest solution tends to be the best one." The wrench in this process is when all things are not equal or similar, which is the case with the composition of all our respective cognitive filters. Maybe similar, but not the same. We venture into this deep water of commitment for various reasons, most of us clinging to what we have in common together, ignoring those things that are nonchalantly labeled as small differences. We write off those differences as being unimportant or insignificant, for they are small compared to the "big love" that two people find in that initial strike of passion for each other. I compare the minimization of differences to "running those yellow lights just before they turn red!" Haha! We talk ourselves into believing all is good when the prize on the other side of that intersection is worth the risk, so to the floor goes the gas pedal. When that prize starts to lose its luster, hesitation to rush through that yellow light sets in, eventually leading to the drift through the red, resulting in getting T-boned by the "insignificant" that was previously ignored! Pay attention to those yellow lights, for eventually, they will need to be addressed. With rational thought and communication, attend to the yellows, process the reds, and proceed when the light goes green. If it doesn't change, make the right turn on red to get off that street. That is a legal move in most states, a move that I failed to make on many occasions simply due to my "need to save" what was on the other side of that intersection.

The differences also can be viewed as being placed in a box that is taped up and written off as a nonfactor. The box of the small stuff lies in wait, only given new life when the box cutters of selfish pride begin to cut away the tape. This increases the visibility of those differences when that box is opened and dumped out on the floor in the name of needing answers and needing validation for blaming the other. The big becomes small, and the small becomes big. It is when the interpretive contrasts of the filters widen in their gap that two people lose sight of the original gravitation to one another. When the battles on the side streets spill over into the main road, the issue of greatest importance in the first place finds it perspective lost. Been there, done that, for sure. Throw in a child or two into the melee, and now you have a "domestic war on steroids" as the combatants are fighting not only for their own self-worth but also the affection of the kid caught in the middle. Gloves are off, and all sense of civility, not always, but often goes into the dumpster. I compare divorce to two people being thrown into the deep end of the pool, each trying to drown the other. Tragically at times in that process, children are pulled in with them and are used as floaties, with the kids being powerless in this "deep end of the pool" struggle for survival. My sister and I were lucky, for when our parents divorced, we were kept out of the water completely. Much respect to my mother and father for that awareness during their "end game" proceedings.

Four metaphors in two paragraphs. Don't say I didn't warn you!

In regards to my own past failed relationships, I have nothing negative to say about any of them. They are good human beings, who at that time, possessed an excellent knack of choosing incredibly charismatic and handsome men! Hahahahaha! Seriously, we were just two humans who met in the wrong place and at the wrong time in our lives. It is in the blessing of my current wife Lori, where boxes of small things were minimal, fully understood, and have been left open and in full view for the past eight years. In eight years, we have slightly raised our voices one time. I call our meeting divine luck and roll with her with a soulful attraction that just simply works. We accept each other without pretense or judgment possibly due to the fact that we finally learned the important lessons just in time before we met, thus creating the perfect landing pad for both of us. I wasn't looking or needing when we met, which is probably one of the main reasons it works. No void to fill, just loving each other in order to add to our lives, not to replace something that was lacking. You often hear others say that marriage is hard work. I suppose that is true, but what tempers that statement is when the relationship is built on the right foundation. Relationships built on shaky ground require a lifetime of remodeling due to the shifting ground beneath. Walls crack, pipes break, and doors and windows won't open and close properly. Fault is irrationally cast about regarding the others framing and decorative shortcomings, when in truth it is the foundation that both parties poured together that is the source of what causes a house to fall in ruin. It's easy to toss around a little blame when you lose sight of what's hidden under the floor coverings. I can honestly say that my present marriage is rather easy, with the effort put out being one of joy and enhancement, not of duty and necessity. Changes are made out of desire, not demand, so little energy is spent on repair. I am truly blessed to have her in this true, life-fulfilling partnership. When I read this to my wife after writing it, her eyes rolled back into her head, then she proceeded to run to the bathroom, audibly ill. Not sure what she ate that caused her nausea, but I'm sure what I read to her gave her comfort in that dispelling moment…must have been the chicken! Haha!

Many enter this, maybe, kinda forever bond for reasons that present challenges from the onset, for rescuers and codependents alike are magnets for dysfunction. Those who derive their self-worth on their ability to "make someone else's life better" or to "transform a tornado into a light summer breeze" often find themselves trapped in the vicious cycle of conflict due to the lack of consistent results of expected change. And yes, once again, I am qualified to comment on this because of my credentials in this area. As mentioned before in this book, my "knight in tinfoil" armor ran amok in the kingdom of Bristolleto, adorning myself with the crown of being able to save someone from themselves. It felt noble at the time, but man, what a shit show of insecurity, arrogance, and ignorance. Through all this was a lesson embedded—that being, the belief that people can only save themselves and should be given 100 percent of the credit for such. We interveners may be able to provide options or even different perspectives, but we do not save others' lives. In my opinion, only the good Lord, first responders, veterans, and doctors get to wear that cape. I've known many that hang their hat on the belief that they are the reason that others get better, or they are saving lives through their heartfelt efforts. There's a complete lack of sanity, for I see those same folks who claim credit for another's improved life trajectory, in turn sneak away from taking responsibility for that other person's struggle after the gallantry. That, folks, is called a total lack of humility. It took me years to learn this lesson, but once I did, that self-imposed pressure to rescue, drastically, if not completely, dissipated. I could write on and on about this topic but will save it for another book. Maybe I'll call it *Poultry Excrement for the Loser's Spiritual Well-Being*. Stay tuned, you just never know…

CHAPTER 7

The Emotional Arsonist

This is another side tidbit that I said that I would address, so here it goes. In my opinion, this may be the most rampant coping mechanism in society today. It is just another perspective on why people are controlling, self-sabotaging, and just all-around passive-aggressive, shit-stirring troublemakers. I see it in our own government where it is on full display, with many citizens being sucked into this inferno to start their own, off-property fires that are started with the same kind of matches. The media is in full match distribution mode, for they lend themselves as a means to divide and conquer. This theory has been around for centuries, for a divided populace is a controlled populace. Imagine if, as a country, we all found a way to live in harmony. The majority would then truly control, and our elected leaders would be forced to do their jobs. They will keep trying to divide us, for their efforts are efficiently hitting on all cylinders. The sheep have found themselves contained by the divisive walls of instigation. Like I said, it has gone on for centuries, and I'm sure, will continue on for centuries to come.

In referring to this concept as it applies to the individual, deception is the trick when it comes to hiding internal insecurities from self and others. When there is a fire burning up the inside of one's own house, these types of personalities will actively set fires in others' yards simply to distract from their own internal struggle. Spending time fighting the blaze in another's yard results is less time having to deal with their own paralyzing issues. They can't control the fire inside, so they go outside to gain some sort of emotional control via conflict with those around them. Instead of smoke and mirrors, it's more like *smoke and fears*. Those undermining fires also create a great deal of smoke, thus making it easier to lose oneself in the billowing ash of the self-denial. This smokescreen also helps in the avoidance of blame for such "arsonistic" acts. Other flame birthers crave the attention of their acts and will wear it as a self-righteous badge. Those are the controllers in this life and are the socialized antisocials of the world. You will also find those that set fire to their own outside buildings in the name of self-sabotage and need for sympathy from their neighbors. In the end, all have the common life theme of having that internal struggle that demands avoidance. Finding belief in the "valuables in your own internal house" is what keeps the outside fires to a minimum and motivates one to focus on the flare-ups inside. Perhaps most of us will find that we have engaged in this type of activity at some time in our lives, most with less destructive motives. Fires will find their way to our own property in due time, so arming ourselves with the retardant of faith, accountability, forgiveness, and kindness will help in the proper management of life's flames. It's when we intentionally engage in that need to avoid our own hard stuff is when that emotional arsonist finds its role on our respective home teams. Unfortunately, it becomes the *star in the line-up* for some and creates that refusal to enter their own burning house in fear of what they find. Courageous are those that thrive. Find your worth and focus on fighting that fire within. It all starts with believing that the sacred belongings in your house are worth the effort and introspection that it takes to battle for what is good. Equip yourself with "good extinguishers" and fight on, people, fight on.

CHAPTER 8

Random Thoughts to Live and Die By

As I move to the wrap-up of this book, I would like to share some other random thoughts and metaphors that have landed on the windshield of my life. There is so much that parallels in this universe, it's just that we seldom notice due to being wrapped up in the tunnel vision of our own troubling issues. Always take the time to take in the beauty, expand your *peripheral vision* and self-check all your devotions from time to time. Never settle as we only get one shot at this unknown number of trips around the sun.

- Where we fight the battles that come roaring down our river of life is up to us. We can attack issues from the middle of that river where the current is strongest, often finding ourselves fighting for air under the surface. Working hard, but not getting any work done, just surviving the torrent of those things that roll and lurk beneath the surface, yearning to pull us under. Through faith, make your way to the safety of the riverbank. Yes, traumatic events will cast us into the deep, but how long we stay out there is of our choosing. Salmon seek to travel the slower water of the river's edge because it's easier. That's where both bears and humans are the most successful in catching their dinner…okay, second thought, don't be like that salmon…

bad idea…just be like the bear, sticking to the shallow to address your survival needs! LOL!

- Give a man a fish, and he'll eat for a day. Teach a man to fish, and he'll then steal all your fishing holes, thus leaving you with no fish. The moral, Give the man a gift card to McDonald's…or give him a fish and tell him to go eat by the bears. Problem solved, fishing hole saved…

- If at first you don't succeed, lower the bar until you do. Lofty, distant goals are useless without breaking the process down to a series of smaller, attainable progress definers. We all seek immediate results, so construct your narrative and course of action with that in mind.

- Do not fear the uncontrollable but control what makes you stronger. Live like the tree that does not fear the storm. Due to its strong roots, it has learned the skill of how to sway in the wind. Be flexible, and be forgiving. The rigid trunk will crack in the gusts presented by the unpredictable.

- The early bird may get the worm, but it will often be the one getting shot by the early hunter. Being first is not always the best option. Also, enjoy every worm because it very well may be your last!

- For much of my life, forgiveness was like taking a ball that someone smashed me in the face with, cleaning it off, and throwing it back in much gentler fashion. It often had more to do with eating that angst in the name of keeping the peace than it had to do with true forgiveness. But it hit me the other day that real, soul-based forgiveness has nothing to do with "the ball." It has *everything* to do with the mitt by which I catch all projectiles that come my way. Anchoring my life in kindness and forgiveness will center on how the actions of others are received, not on how I react. Clarity now demands action, but man, the "lightning bolt" of this revelation was really, really empowering.

- "To commingle expectations with wishes is to give life to those things that stand to cause the most grief. To wish is to hope, with nothing lost if desires regarding others' actions do not come to fruition. It is in the web of expectation where control is surrendered, and insight is lost to the spiral of one's own emotional spike over others' plights. Following others down those rabbit holes, I now avoid, as those destructive, underground "garden of life raiding rodent tunnels" lead to nowhere that is anywhere near a productive solution. Fruitless emotion and a disservice to your own sense of control—this stumbling emotional dance of expectation can be for all involved.

- "*To blame is to surrender.* Once we blame others for our emotional situation, we surrender all control to that person. And yes, blaming is different from clarifying accountability via boundary-setting. Boundary-setting affectively removes the surrendering component of this *blame game*.

- "Manage your emotional remotes. Many of us hand out emotional remotes like politicians hand out promises, resulting in too much control being given to our employers, friends, strangers, family members, and aforementioned politicians. Let's say one of the above mentioned parties commits a not-so-positive act. Our initial reaction may be one of disappointment, anger, or betrayal, which is natural. But how long do we allow that feeling to run on our track? Hanging on to the emotion associated is like giving out that remote to the person that offended. You don't control them, so why do you give them the control of your own happiness? Gather those remotes, safely stow them away, and forge on. Our control is our choice."

- "Treat others as individuals with free will, not as a member of a group or larger population. How many times do we make assumptions based on who others associate with and not on their individual identity? Same applies, vice versa, as individuals need to see themselves as responsible for their own actions, regardless of the mob-mentality post onto which they hitch their accountability horse. We have completely lost the *me* and fallen back on the *we* when it comes to accountability for our bad behavior."

- "Don't buy a bucking horse and expect the horse to quit bucking just because you think you have a nicer saddle." For all out there that have found their mate in the "Cheaters Are Us" yellow pages, don't be disappointed when at some point down the trail that horse decides to toss you and your fancy saddle into the cactus patch. Bottom line is, you really aren't as special as you think. And yes, I have spent much time in my past picking cactus thorns out of my sorry, rescuer saddle-riding, arse!"
- Kindness is free…unless you borrow it from the kitty of being a victim. Stand firm in your convictions for self. At the end of the battle, whether won or lost, you will not have surrendered any ground. Forgiveness is kindness.
- You can lead a horse to water, but when you try and hold their head under to make 'em drink, you will probably get kicked in the face. The moral, *ride a camel. They need less water.*
- Life is not a popularity contest. Needing to be the most liked places one in a constant quest for outer gratification, often times resulting in a "at any cost" campaign. Rest on your own kind actions, and if those actions are pure in intent, it is admiration you will naturally receive.

As I move to wrap up this complex, metaphorical "water system" project, I am reminded of a story I heard in 1979 regarding a preacher in a small Texas church. His parishioners would notice every morning that he would drop a dollar in the offering box prior to his sermon. When asked about why he would put dollar in his own offering container, the preacher replied, "Every Sunday, I make sure to put my own dollar in the church till. By doing this, I know that regardless of what the congregation offers up, I know I will at least have one dollar to collect at the end of the service. At the end of the day, my offering box will never be empty." So true is this when searching for any lasting change in this life. I have come to embrace this mindset over the span of my life, for I do not expect others to fill my own "church till" in regards to any life task I may set my sights on. For many years, I looked for outside sources to validate my life, falling short in almost every instance, good or bad. This was even more prevalent in my desire for something better in regards to my search for my own middle lane of serenity. In retrospect, the best things in my life are those I found in the giving of my time and effort. The twenty-five years spent volunteering as a high school baseball coach and the past nine years with the nonprofit, has not been without great financial and personal sacrifice. Through it all, however, I regret none of it, for the lessons learned and relationships forged are far beyond any financial value. You cannot put a price on beautiful, everlasting humility and appreciation. Looking back, when I first started Base Camp 40, it was clearly a dedication to do something epic and something that was uniquely special in its own way. In the face of crushing financial cost, I never questioned why for

God had a plan. That is what faith means to me. I am somewhat of a "go big or go home" type of player in this world of charitable giving, for if I am going to make a difference in this life, I'm going to give it a chance to be a lasting one. I now find myself humbled and blessed to have had a role in the birth of a grassroots movement that now has a beautiful spirit of its own. I now look forward to the next life chapter; that being my future literary works. The Bear Rock Project honors the lives of my late father, Rock, and my companion of fifteen years, my dog, Bear, who crossed the rainbow bridge last year.

I am also looking forward to my other personal project in building Scarlett's Way, a mission to give back to Shriners Hospital, and to those families whose child has been diagnosed with fibular hemimelia. My biggest hero is my four-year-old step-granddaughter, Scarlett Whitmore, who at nine months of age had her lower right leg amputated due to this condition. She now rambles on with her prosthetic, knocking down any limiting wall set before her. She is another source of spiritual strength in my life, for sure.

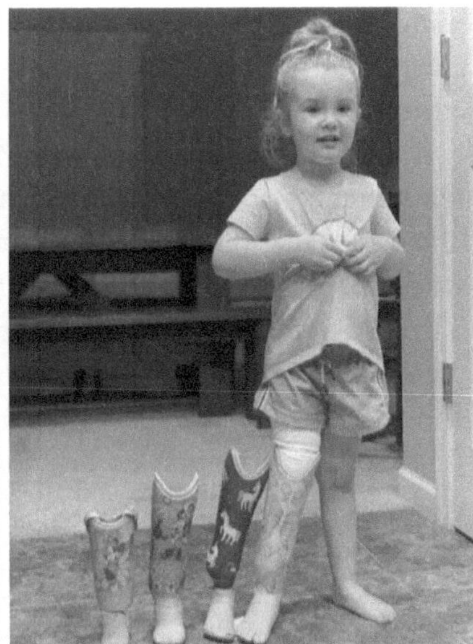

Scarlett and her "arsenal of leggies!"

At the end of the day, I can rest easy, for my life has been blessed with good intent. My "dollar offering" has been spiritually returned a millionfold by so many. Just having the opportunity to give back is a blessing in itself.

It is in that drive, even through all the self-manufactured turmoil of my past, that I discovered the motivation for this *Absolution Tap* project. It was the rise of my rejection of settling for the constant struggle in my life. I not only needed but, more importantly, wanted something better. I'm sure many will have read this book and been less than convinced of its practicality, for one reason or another, That is okay, for as I mentioned at the onset, I am not advocating this approach for anybody. I am simply sharing what I found in this haystack of life-balancing solutions. I know this process has changed my core, revealing much of what I had avoided and much that I chose to not include in this book. It has given me validation that these words are more than a creative ensemble of metaphors meant to entertain others. There is meaning behind this madness, and it's meaning that comes without the expectation of acceptance from others. That is the purity of this project. Its success has already been achieved in my mind, prior to the sale of a single book. Critics will clamor, but their perspective has no place in defining the worth I place on this literary effort.

In review of the contents of this book, if I had to sum it up in a few sentences, it would be this. Change comes at the top and bottom of our life tank model. How we interpret or filter life events, and how we dispense the end product to self and others is of most importance. There is so much in between that sculpts what we create; lead by that life-defining cause and effect. We are never bound by any mindset, and with hard, dedicated work, we can get up and change our seat. I have been my biggest enemy, and with God's ever-present hand to lead, have become my strongest ally. Through the soulful liberation of forgiveness of self and others, I have found my new way of living without fear and trepidation and have lightened the impact of my depressive swings. Whatever comes my way, I will be okay, for in the end, there is salvation beyond comprehension waiting. "I shall not judge, for I do not hold the highest throne." I will live out my life with this mantra, a life that will hold more tragedy and triumph, for that *is* life. The more you love, the greater you will feel that loss. What I have gained in loving towers over the painful loss that waits for all of us. I will live with that appreciation for having that chance to love and will do all I can to ensure that any grief in loss is due to the grandeur of the gift that will be forever cherished, not the "after the fact" regrets to be rued and given the power to torment. So true is this in regards to what I lay before myself. Getting to this place on this "trek up the mountain" where I truly forgive myself has been grueling, but I have made it all the same, and now have found a reliable and productive weapon in my struggle with depression. The "ghost," I can safely say, now has a face, and no longer roams my "ballroom" to destructively cut into my life dance without detection or without reprisal.

You are worth the effort, you are worth the challenge, and you are worth the spoils of true absolution. Frolic in that clean water that is always present at the top of your tanks. Therein lies the purpose-defining gift of this existence.

God bless you all in your journey in the process of maintaining the good water in your life tanks. Clarity awaits those that do not fear the open eye and those who devoutly embrace the forgiven, humbled heart.

The End

Born in 1964 and raised in a rural farm setting near Grand Junction, Colorado, Paul Bristol has made his hometown his current residence for the last twenty-seven years. He currently resides with his wife Lori, and their "fur ball" children—Lyric (dog/fairy princess) and two cats, Logan (spawn of Satan!) and Zoey (Black Ops/secret agent!). Having no children of his own, Paul considers these animals as being "his kids" with his heart also being stolen by his step-grandchildren in Bakersfield, California. Sharing that love for the gift of nature is also a common binding agent for Paul and Lori. Both are avid hunters (and yes, Paul graciously admits that Lori is the best freezer filler of the two) who see the hunt as a gift and a harvest to be deeply respected.

Currently working as a railroad engineer for the past twenty-six years, Paul has dedicated the last nine years of his life to the charitable organization that he formed after the passing of his father in 2010.

Whistler Entertainment Inc./DBA Base Camp 40—Warriors in The Wild. "We can never rightfully repay the debt of freedom that our service men and women have sacrificed their lives for. What we offer is simply a drop in the bucket in comparison to what they have given to us here at home." Rediscovering his clarity of faith has been a game changer and a lifesaver but is never something that he forces upon others. "I can only try to be an example for others in how I reconstructed those lasting changes in my life narrative. You are never too old to search for that better way." Through writing poetry (wannabe songs, he calls them!), Paul states he has found his release, with the *Absolution Tab* being the culmination of all his creative works. "If it helps one person gain a small foothold in their struggle, all is worth the time and effort. Okay, maybe two people, for the one person has already been helped, that being myself. The best gift to self is undoubtedly found in giving to others. That is the indelible lesson that this life has taught me."

9 781662 406072